Nigel Adams

· Silver Link Library of Railway M

RAILWAY MODELLING REALISM

An aspirational guide

· Nigel Adams & Kevin Cartwright ·

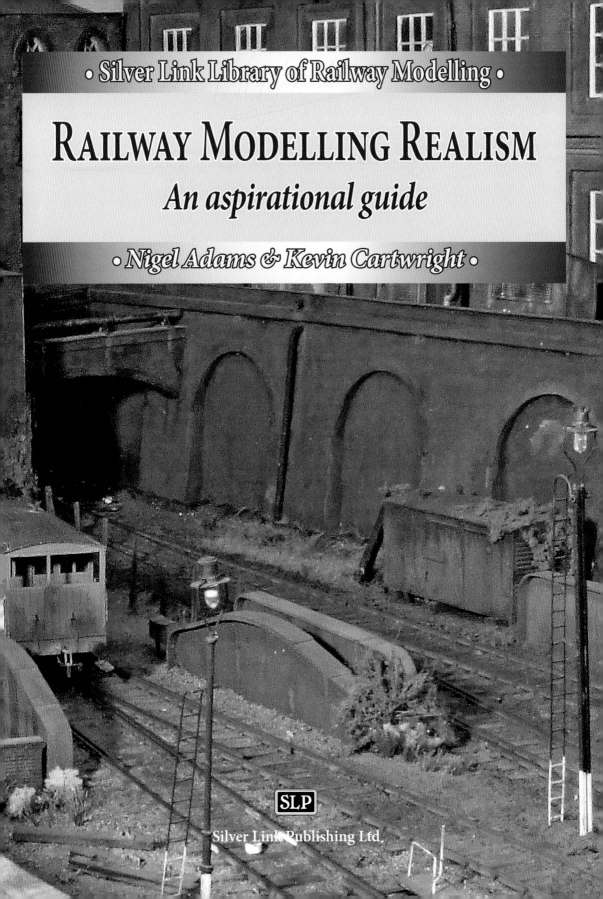

· Silver Link Library of Railway Modelling ·

RAILWAY MODELLING REALISM
An aspirational guide

· *Nigel Adams & Kevin Cartwright* ·

SLP

Silver Link Publishing Ltd

First published in 2012

British Library Cataloguing in Publication Data

A catalogue record for this book is available from the British Library.

ISBN 978 1 85794 405 1

Silver Link Publishing Ltd
The Trundle
Ringstead Road
Great Addington
Kettering
Northants NN14 4BW

Tel/Fax: 01536 330588
email: sales@nostalgiacollection.com
Website: www.nostalgiacollection.com

Printed and bound in the Czech Republic

Photographs credited to Ray Ruffell are
© Silver Link Publishing Ltd

Half title: **Kevin Cartwright's 'Stodmarsh'.** *Craig Tiley, courtesy of Model Rail*

Title page: **'Gas Works' by the Yeovil Model Railway Group.** *Bob Alderman*

Below: **A view of '82G'.** *Tony Wright, courtesy of British Railway Modelling*

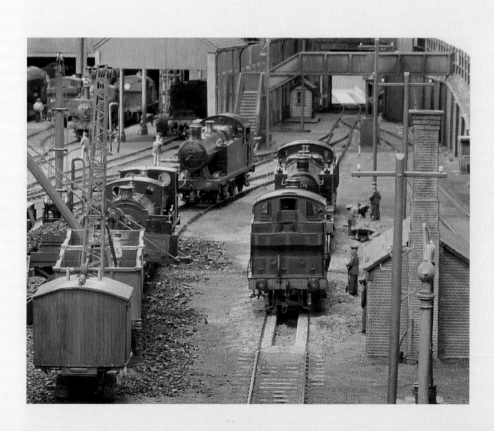

Contents

Introduction   7

1   Ideas for layouts   10
2   Prototype scenic detail   24
3   Realistic model scenic detail   40
4   Layout gallery   61
5   Building prototype layouts   123
6   Somewhere to work   141

Index   143

A scene on Kevin Cartwright's 'Stodmarsh'. *Craig Tiley, Courtesy of Model Rail*

Acknowledgements

I could not have written this book on my own and I particularly want to thank the contributors who have readily written about their layouts and provided photographs and plans. I also want to thank those who have provided prototype photographs.

The book could not have been written at all without Kevin Cartwright's input. He is a superb modeller of prototype layouts and rolling stock, which is something I could never aspire to if I tried. Not only that, he paints his own backscenes from the prototype as shown on his 'Brixham Bay' layout. As the idea for the book was to compare the prototype scene with the model scene, Kevin's input was absolutely vital. He wrote Chapter 5 and provided me with a lot of other material too.

I have had the pleasure of knowing Kevin and his wife Judy for many years by seeing them on the 'exhibition circuit', and value their friendship enormously. Thanks are also due to Judy for typing Kevin's input and emailing it to me as they live in Brixham and Celia and I live in Mid Wales.

Special thanks are due to Sarah Ventry, who typed my input into this book; to Doris Southgate, who typed the captions, and to Lawrie Bowles, who proofread the text. I am also extremely grateful to Ray Reid, who used his computer skills to supplement my very basic ability. My elder son Justin also helped in this respect, and he also regularly operates my layouts at exhibitions.

I owe a great debt to Steve Flint, John Emerson, Tony Wright and Ben Jones for so readily agreeing to let me use plans and photographs previously used in *Railway Modeller*, *British Railway Modelling* and *Model Rail* magazines.

Thanks are also due to the members of Tywyn & District Model Railway Club, of which I was a founder member in November 2001, for their support and friendship. We are only a small club but it is good to meet regularly with like-minded people.

Finally, I have been married to Celia for 48 years and she has supported and encouraged me in the hobby all that time. I owe her an immense debt of gratitude for that. I also exhibit at quite a few exhibitions each year, which, because of where we live, often means being away from home from Friday to Monday, and she never complains.

Our older grandson (now aged 11) said he had 'gone off trains', but in 2011 he had regained enough interest to come and help operate my layout at the Leamington exhibition. I look forward to our younger grandson (only 2 at the moment!) and his little sister (7 months old at the time of writing) also showing interest in the future.

Railway modelling can be a great family hobby if the children are encouraged. That is why I often run models of Toby (complete with face!), Thomas and Percy on my layout at exhibitions. Sometimes it is obvious that the purists don't like it, but I have no intention of stopping.

It is to my wife, my two sons, my daughter-in-law and my grandchildren that I dedicate this book.

Introduction

Some people have the space, the funds and the time to build a large layout, and we read about superb examples of such layouts from time to time in the model railway magazines. Some such layouts have been the subject of a book in their own right and have encouraged other modellers to try their best to build their own examples. Three examples of such layouts are 'The Buckingham Branch', built by the late Rev Peter Denny, which was the subject of two books published by Wild Swan Publications Ltd, *Peter Denny's Buckingham Branch Lines 1945-1967* (1993) and *Peter Denny's Buckingham Branch Lines 1967-1993* (1994); 'The Greenlane & Hillside Railway', built by Robert Preston Hendry in his attic and the subject of the book *The Living Model Railway* written by his son Robert Powell Hendry and published by Silver Link Publishing Ltd in 1994; and, more recently, Pete Waterman's book about his 'Leamington Spa' layout, *Just Like The Real Thing*, published by Ian Allan Publishing in 2009.

Most of us do not have the resources to build a large, realistic layout on our own, and this is where model railway clubs come in. Some have built superb large layouts where a group of members with a common interest have got together. Two examples from recent years are 'Chee Tor', by the Manchester Model Railway Society, and 'Chiltern Green', from the Model Railway Club in London. As it happens, both are in 2mm scale. Many more examples can be seen at exhibitions up and down the country and in magazines.

The secret of building convincing layouts – of whatever size – is to concentrate on producing something that looks prototypical, and this can be done in many different scales, gauges and layout sizes. For example, if space is a problem you can concentrate on a particular area of the prototype and build a convincing model of, say, an engine shed and its surroundings; a diesel refuelling point; a goods yard; factory sidings; a small station; or a dockside railway. Whatever the choice, and whatever the size of your layout, the same principles apply. You can choose standard gauge or narrow gauge, and any scale, although if you do not have much space it is unlikely that you will be able to accommodate the very large scales. Chapter 1 gives some ideas for layouts.

One way of building a satisfying layout is to concentrate on scenic detail, which I think is so important in creating a convincing layout. Therefore Chapter 2 consists principally of photographs of prototype scenic detail, split into the various headings as outlined above.

Chapter 3 is similar, but the photographs are of layouts where convincing and realistic prototypical scenes have been portrayed.

Chapter 4 is described as a 'Layout Gallery', a format that has proved popular in my previous two books for Silver Link Publishing, *Layouts for Limited Spaces*, published in 1996, and *More Layouts for Limited Spaces*, published in 2010. Perhaps its popularity it is not surprising because in each of the model railway magazines that is exactly what is done every month – a number of layouts of varying types, sizes and gauges are described with photographs, plans, etc. Due to space limitations the majority of layouts in this chapter are only described very briefly, the text supported by a layout plan, some photographs and other brief details, but a few are described in more detail.

Chapter 5 was written by Kevin Cartwright for those who wish to build a specific prototype layout. He describes how this was done for five layouts, 'Seahouses', 'Stodmarsh' and 'Ventnor West', all in O gauge, 'Arley', a Severn Valley Railway layout he is building in OO gauge, having already made some of the buildings and a superb model of the bridge, and 'Brixham Bay', in N gauge. Again, there are many photographs of prototypes and models. Kevin and his wife Judy are well known on the 'exhibition circuit', and you may well have seen them with their 'Seahouses' or 'Stodmarsh' layouts, which have been shown at many exhibitions over the last few years.

Chapter 6 is really an afterthought! Early in 2011 my wife and I moved from a cottage thought to date from the 17th century to a 20th-century bungalow. My modelling in the cottage was done in the third bedroom – of which I had sole use – but there were disadvantages, the main one being that the stairs were very steep, and taking a layout to an exhibition meant that it had to be carried up and down them. Having got it downstairs, depending on the weather, it had to be crated for transport in the living room if wet, or on the pavement if dry, because the garden was not attached to the cottage! The stock boxes, exhibition boxes and the tool box had also to be carried up and down the stairs. All this is not what you want when you get back from a full day or weekend at an exhibition!

One of the attractions of the bungalow, apart from the lack of stairs, was that it had a 12 feet by 8 feet shed in the garden with power

to it. It was not in good condition, but Chapter 6 tells how it was made into a very comfortable modelling room, with photographs of it as it is now.

Whatever the size of your layout, I believe there is something immensely satisfying in creating one that is either based on an actual prototype or looks extremely convincing but is not a model of an actual location. Many modellers have produced extremely convincing layouts that are not of real locations, and very often such layouts have an imaginary history to 'justify their existence'. One such layout is the 'Craig & Mertonford Railway', built a long time ago by the late P. D. Hancock, who died in 2011.

I also well remember 'Borchester Market' being exhibited at the Model Railway Club's 1979 exhibition at Central Hall, Westminster. I had built an OO layout, 'Brookhurst', with my elder son Justin to show what father and son could do together with readily available track, rolling stock, buildings, etc. For some reason it was popular at exhibitions, and was exhibited at Westminster in that year. On two or three occasions Justin and I were invited behind the scenes at 'Borchester Market' before the exhibition opened, and it was fascinating. Its builder, the late Frank Dyer, deserved all the plaudits the layout received. I understand that the layout is now on the exhibition circuit again under new ownership. I look forward to seeing it again.

An example of model scenic detail on the author's 'Bottrill Street Yard (Mk 1)' layout in O gauge. *Martin Hewitt*

Finally in this Introduction I wanted to include a photograph of a toolbox. This may seem rather odd, but in a sense it explains why I am so interested in railways and model railways. My father was born in Swindon in 1912 and his father was a timekeeper in the GWR Works. My mother's father also worked there as a carriage-maker.

My father matriculated to London University twice but could not go because his parents could not afford to pay the fees and support him. When he left school he therefore started with the GWR as an apprentice fitter and turner. Whatever their trades, all apprentices had to make their own toolbox, and the one in the photograph is the one my father made.

In 1938 the GWR sacked 1,300 employees on the basis of 'last in, first out', and my father, in common with many others, went to work in the growing car industry in Oxford. He began work in the toolroom at the Pressed Steel Company Co Ltd. Many years later, in 1966, Pressed Steel merged with BMC to form British Motor Holdings Ltd, then in 1968 that company merged with Leyland Motors to form British Leyland Ltd. My father became a foreman in 1941 and eventually retired from the company in 1977 as Tooling Manager, having been Toolroom Superintendent and Nightshift Manager for the whole factory in between. In 1984 he had to go into a care home and he gave me his toolbox.

My younger son has two sons and he recently asked me if he could have the toolbox

On the right is my father's toolbox, which he made when he was an apprentice in the GWR Works at Swindon. The photograph was taken in 1992 when I was Vicar of Holy Cross Church at Wyken in Coventry. The fourth bedroom in the Vicarage was my 'modelling room'. My workbench was an old computer desk, while the chest of drawers dates back to 1970! *Author*

when I died, saying that he wanted to be able to pass it on to one of his sons in the future, and I have gladly agreed to that. The toolbox is now almost 80 years old and it is good to know that it will be passed on to future generations in years to come.

With a father serving his apprenticeship at the GWR's Swindon Works, working there until 1938, two grandfathers who worked there for many years, and a great uncle who worked out of Weymouth as a guard and let me ride with him regularly when I was young, it is not surprising that I am so interested in railways and model railways!

1 ∘ Ideas for layouts

Magazines are a superb source of ideas for layouts. Clearly you cannot fill your home with piles of magazines, but you can be selective and keep the articles that interest you. I do this and now have four large folders full of articles that I have removed from magazines. They serve as my ideas library when I am thinking about a new layout or looking for ideas for a particular scenic aspect of one I am building.

With a few exceptions the articles listed below are fairly recent and you may be able to get hold of the relevant magazines from the back numbers department of the publication concerned. Failing that, have a look at the second-hand magazine stands at exhibitions or at preserved railways. For example, the South Devon Railway has a good supply kept in a railway coach at Totnes; they are kept in date order for each magazine so it is easy to find the one you want.

For many years I have been a great fan of building layouts depicting engine sheds or motive power depots. My most recent layout is an O-gauge model of a diesel refuelling point/stabling point. It has one point and is 56 inches long, with a small cassette area 8 inches long, making a total length of 64 inches (see page 121).

Tywyn Model Railway Club, of which I am Chairman, has built three engine shed layouts. 'Cheapside Depot' (OO gauge) was built on the bottom shelf of a two-tier coffee table bought in the local Red Cross shop for £5. It is called 'Cheapside' because everything used in its construction was second-hand! It measures 48 by 18 inches.

'Worthington Shed' (O gauge) was built on one of three baseboards the club was given after the death of one of its founder members. He had built three boards measuring 48 by 32 inches on which to build his new O-gauge

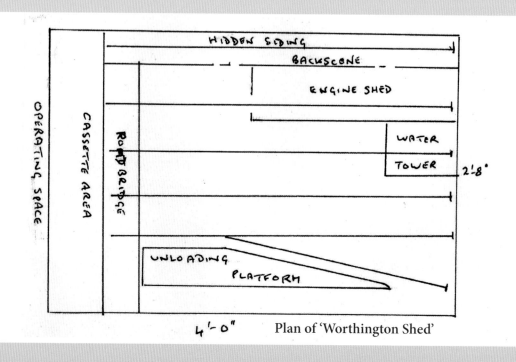

Plan of 'Worthington Shed'

layout, but sadly he died before he could start to build it.

Finally, 'Neptune Road Depot' (OO gauge) was also built on one of the three baseboards mentioned above, and was based on a layout plan that appeared in *Railway Modeller* some years ago. It has now been broken up.

Some of the other layouts I have built are described in my previous book, *More Layouts for Limited Spaces*.

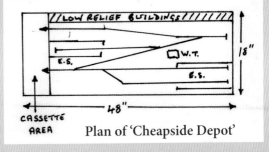

Plan of 'Cheapside Depot'

I also have two Gn15 layouts. One is entirely fictitious, built on a board of 48 by 24 inches for ease of transport to and from exhibitions and for storage in my shed. This is called 'The Works' and depicts the entrance to a works with a two-road engine shed nearby. The other is called 'Iron Street Sheds'; it is built on an ironing board measuring 55 by 16 inches, and fits into the back of my Skoda Fabia with the rear squab folded down. It is based on a photograph in a book written about the 15-inch-gauge railway built by Sir Arthur Heywood in the grounds of his home in the early 20th century. The book is called *Sir Arthur Heywood and the 15-inch Gauge Railway*, written by Mark Smithers and published by Plateway Press.

An overall view of Cheapside Depot in the Tywyn MRC clubroom. Using the bottom shelf of the coffee table as the 'baseboard' gives the opportunity for the top shelf to be used to mount the fascia and for storage of equipment at an exhibition, as seen in the drawing. *Author*

I have also built a layout in O gauge measuring 90 by 22 inches called 'Tywyn Railway Preservation Society'. This is another 'dodge' you can adopt if you do not want to build a model of an actual location. If you visit a preserved railway, whether standard or narrow gauge, you will see a complete mixture of rolling stock and locomotives. I have been a working volunteer on the Talyllyn Railway since 1983, and of course it is important that we still have the original two locomotives, *Talyllyn* and *Dolgoch*, as well as the four original four-wheel coaches and Van 5, the brake-van. In addition, we have four more

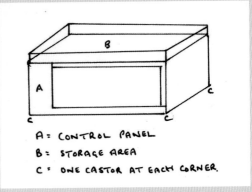

A = CONTROL PANEL
B = STORAGE AREA
C = ONE CASTOR AT EACH CORNER.

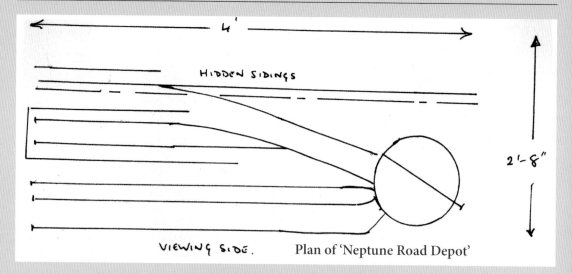

VIEWING SIDE.   Plan of 'Neptune Road Depot'

David Church and his two sons operate 'Neptune Road Depot' at the 2009 Tywyn MRC exhibition. The layout has since been scrapped. *Paul Gunn*

steam locomotives, one of which we built in our works, and four diesels, two of which have been completely rebuilt. We have also bought two more diesels fairly recently – so even the preserved railway changes. This variety of rolling stock is even more marked on many standard-gauge preserved lines, especially when there is a Gala Day with visiting locos. Also, people who purchase a loco often ask a preserved railway if it can be given a home and used there. Therefore if you do not want to model a particular prototype and prefer to run whatever locos and rolling stock you like, producing a layout that portrays a preserved railway (fictitious or otherwise) will meet your needs.

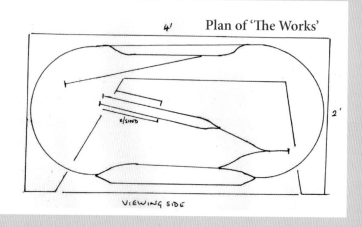

Plan of 'The Works'

VIEWING SIDE

Above: An overall view of 'The Works' in the author's garden. *Author*

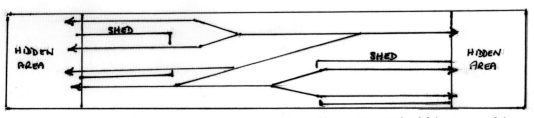

Plan of 'Iron Street Sheds' (not to scale).

Left: An overall view of 'Iron Street Sheds', showing how the ironing board is used to support the layout. It measures 51 inches by 14.5 inches and, when folded, the ironing board measures 57 inches by 17 inches. *Author*

Right: A view looking down over 'Iron Street Sheds' showing how the fiddle yard is accessed from all roads – as it is at the other end of the baseboard. *Author*

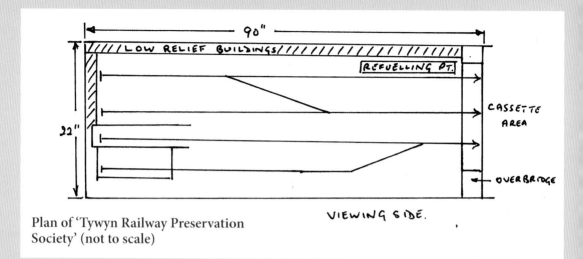

Plan of 'Tywyn Railway Preservation Society' (not to scale)

Other steam and diesel depot layouts are listed in the accompanying table.

Steam depots				
'Sedgemore Road'	OO	RM	Nov 2004	Chas May
'Sykes Bridge'	O	BRM	Apr 2005 and 2008	Jeff Nicholls
'Tolcarn Engine Shed'	O	BRM	Sep 2001	Terry Yeend
St Marnock	O	BRM	Jun 2009	Mike Bissett
		RM	Oct 2010	
Diesel depots				
'Hanging Hill TMD'	OO	BRM	Jan/Feb 2008	Clive Mortimer
'Moore Street TMD'	OO	RM	Dec 2010	Dominic Moore and Peter Thornton
'Hendre Lane Stabling Point'	OO	RM	Nov 2010	Marc Smith
'Hydraulic Heaven'	G1	BRM	Jul 2009	Steve Harrod

The enormous variety of industrial buildings, locomotives and rolling stock found on industrial systems permits the maximum use of your imagination in filling the baseboards as against – if I can put it this way – the basic buildings usually found on a country branch line, for example station, signal box, goods shed, small loco shed, etc. This is particularly true at the present time with a great variety of industrial buildings available, including those from American suppliers such as Walthers. You are only limited by your imagination!

If you are looking for ideas for such layouts, I can thoroughly recommend two books. *Model Railway Planning and Design Handbook* was compiled by Steve Flint, who is now editor of *Railway Modeller* magazine, with contributions by Paul Lunn, Neil Ripley, Ken Gibbons and Jack Burnard. In particular, Neil's contribution entitled 'Industrial, Dockland

Locos on shed on the author's 'Tywyn Railway Preservation Society' layout. *Author*

An overall view looking across 'Tywyn Railway Preservation Society'. *Author*

Two views taken at Bodmin on the occasion of the railway's 2011 Gala Weekend. Here steam and diesel locos are side by side, and there is a considerable number of years between the dates when they were built. *Both author*

Above: Machynlleth engine shed is seen in steam days on 23 July 1966 with a 'Standard 4' on shed. *Ray Ruffell*

Above: After steam ceased, Machynlleth became a diesel refuelling point. Some of the steam-era buildings survive, including the one above. There is a lot of detail here for those who wish to model such a location. *Author*

Left: This is Machynlleth depot as it is now under the control of Arriva Trains Wales Ltd. *Author*

and Light Railway Themes' is very relevant. Neil and Jack are also contributors to this book.

The other book is *Building Micro Layouts*, by Paul Lunn. As the title suggests, is all about the building of very small layouts and there are many good ideas in it. Both books are published by Santona Publications, now owned by Book Law Publications, who can be seen with their stand at many of the larger exhibitions.

Ideas for industrial-type layouts are seen regularly in the model railway press and listed in the accompanying table are examples divided into various categories.

Yards				
'Windmill Road' (wagon repair depot)	OO	RM	Nov 2009	Ashley Toone
'Widnes Vine Yard'	OO	Hornby	Sept 2010	Wirral Finescale Modellers
'Eagle Lane'	OO	RM	Feb 2009	Richard Coleman
'Neptune Street Yard'	OO	RM	Feb 2008	Anthony Bilton
'Cripps Bottom Yard'	OO	Hornby	Oct 2010	Keith Armitage
Docks				
'Overlord'	OO	BRM	Jan 1996	Chris Mead
'Chatham Docks'	O	RM	Jun 2005	Chatham MRC
'Carters Dock'	OO	RM	Nov 2007	Graham Hand
Factories and industrial				
'Mossop Road'	EM	RM	Sep 2007	Andrew Wright
'Egypt Brewery'	EM	RM	Jul 2010	Paul Cope
'The Brickworks'	0-14	RM	Sep 1998	Arthur Budd
'The Pipe Yard'	0-16.5	RM	May 2009	David Lenton
Sidings				
'Jubilee Sidings'	EM	RM	Mar 2006	Dave Tailby
'Saxlingham'	EM	RM	Sep 2007	Dave Tailby
'Wintringham Haven'	EM	RM	Jun 2006	Jeff Taylor
'Alloa Goods'	EM	BRM	Mar 2003	Jeff Taylor
Collieries				
'Houghton Colliery'	G1	RM	Apr 2005	Jack Burnard

You can also get ideas from articles about prototype locations, and such ideas are not new. In the April 1980 edition of *Model Railway Constructor* Peter Kazmierczak wrote an article entitled 'Locomotive yards – realistic operations in a small space'.

In the article he said that even motive power depots take up a surprising amount of space to model effectively and, from a scenic point of view, 'the actual shed can dominate the layout to create an unbalanced scene'. His suggestion was that a 'locomotive yard' can be fitted into a small space, can feature a wide variety of locomotive types and can be worked to a timetable. It is also often sited in a cramped situation. In steam days these yards enabled locos to be turned and watered, and in today's world diesel locos are refuelled there. The main purpose of these facilities was and is to enable a quick turn-round of locos. The purpose of the article was to suggest the locomotive yard as a possible layout, which in OO gauge is very achievable even in modern

houses where space is at a premium. I have built a layout of such a site – mine is imaginary but, I hope, prototypical (see 'The Stabling Point' on page 121).

Peter Kazmierczak suggested two London prototypes: King's Cross Loco Yard and Ranelagh Bridge Sidings. The former was situated alongside the entrance to Gasworks Tunnel and consisted of five sidings; the turntable was removed in the mid-1960s. The latter was just outside Paddington station,

Above: A general view of 'The Works Yard' as drawn by Peter F. Winding in 1947.

Left: The works yard and shed buildings looking north from the engine hoist.

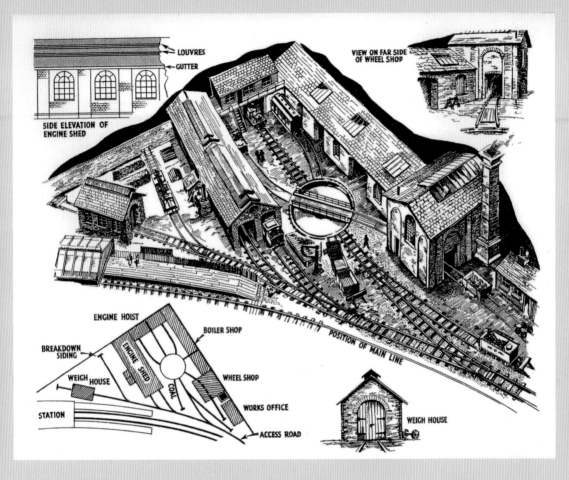

Above: A drawing and plan showing how effectively the yard can be housed in a corner.

Below: The facade of the erecting shop at New Cross Gate.

Peter F. Winding's drawing and plan of an adaptation of the New Cross Gate roundhouse, accommodated in the corner of a layout.

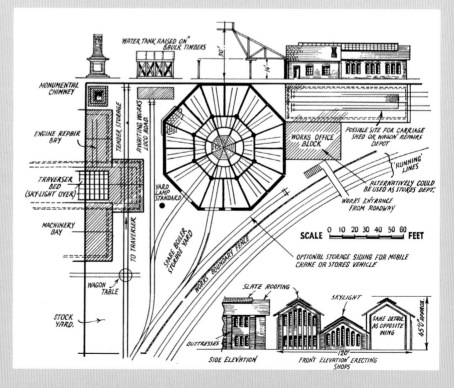

south of the main line, and had six sidings; its turntable had also been removed. Peter felt that 'with a little adaptation' both these yards could be built in 4mm scale on a baseboard 6 feet by 2 feet, and could also form part of a large layout. St Pancras and Liverpool Street also had similar facilities, the latter including a loco washing point.

One of the articles in my ideas library that still gives me inspiration goes back 53 years. It appeared in the July and October 1958 editions of *Model Railway Constructor* and is entitled 'The Works Yard'. It was written by Peter F. Winding, who I believe was the draughtsman with Ian Allan Ltd, publisher of the magazine.

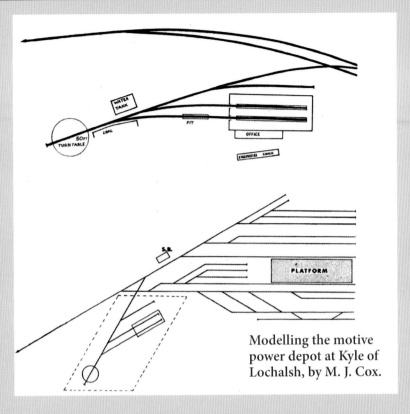

Modelling the motive power depot at Kyle of Lochalsh, by M. J. Cox.

He writes: 'The prototype for this model was the historic depot at New Cross Gate, which served as a repair works and locomotive shed from 1839 to 1947…' The practice of railways doing a great deal of repair, maintenance and renewal work in their own workshops was common until 50-60 years ago, and still is on preserved railways such as the Talyllyn Railway. Clearly it would be impossible to model something vast like Swindon Works, but some of the older works were very small and would be suitable for quite modest layouts.

To quote from Peter Winding's article again: 'The important thing about [the proposed plan] is the yard, which stimulates an interest by being operational. The works buildings are, in effect, only dummies, skilfully arranged to encompass the yard, and to concentrate the spectator's interest within that sphere.'

Peter Winding also wrote an article about New Cross Gate in the December 1978 issue

of *Railway World*, also published by Ian Allan. I am very grateful to Nick Lerwill of Ian Allan Publishing Ltd for readily agreeing that Peter Winding's drawings could be used in this book.

In looking through some old magazines while visiting our son's home, I came across an old *Model Railway News* (which ceased publication long ago). It contained a short article suggesting that the motive power depot at Kyle of Lochalsh would be a good one to model. I agree. It had two roads leading off the turntable road, and near the shed there was an old LNWR sleeping car, presumably being used as a 'bothy' by the staff. I reproduce the plan here. The very short article was written by M. J. Cox, and if he reads this I am most grateful for it because it is a very good example of what I am trying to say.

As an acknowledged fan of layouts featuring engine sheds and works, I find them absolutely fascinating and, as I said earlier, they continue to give me ideas.

In the table below are listed articles on prototype, terminus, branch-line, narrow-gauge and continuous layouts.

Prototype layouts				
'Banbury NW'	EM	MRJ	No 28, 1989	(The late) David Ratcliff
'Farewell Romsey'	OO	Hornby	Feb 2009	David Barker
'Totnes'	N	BRM	Jan 2009	John Birkett Smith
Termini				
'Dormston Terminus'	O	RM	Feb 2009	Stephen Shepherd
'Stoke Fleming'	O	RM	Nov 1998	Alan Searle
'Bridport Town'	0-16.5	RM	Dec 2010	David Taylor
Branch lines				
'Brixworth Station'	OO	RM	Oct 2008	George Woodcock
'Summers Town'	OO	RM	Sep 2007	Jeff Taylor
'Llwynmawr'	P4	BRM	Sep 1995	Rex Ashton
'Llansilin'	Scale 4	BRM	Sep 2003	Rex Ashton
Narrow gauge				
'Moorton Bottom Yard'	009	RM	May 2007	Paul Windle
'Blackwood Valley Railway'	0-16.5	RM	Feb 2010	P. J. Sanders
Continuous layouts				
'Tetley Mills'	OO	BRM	Jan 2011	Dave Shakespeare
'South Pimlico'	OO	Hornby	Nov 2009	Colin Whitelock

Another source of ideas for layouts is an exhibition programme. Many of the larger exhibitions – for example the Warley National, The Gauge O Guild, the Stafford exhibition – include some layout plans in the exhibition guide. Again, I cut them out and keep the ones that appeal to me; they take up very little space and are a good resource when thinking about a new layout.

Two examples are quoted. The first is 'Melbury Loops', an O-gauge 7mm/ft layout built by the Milton Railway Group in the late 1970s; I think I first saw it at the Model Railway Club's 1979 exhibition. It depicted

Plan of 'Melbury Loops'

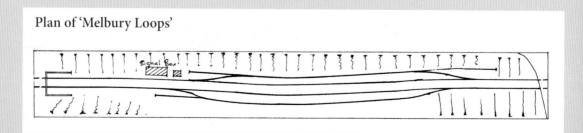

a double-track main line running through countryside with a passing loop for each track. It was built to enable trains to run at realistic speeds without the distraction of station halts, shunting and engine turning; these functions were carried out in the hidden loops behind the scenes. Because the layout incorporated two passing loops, spectators' interest was maintained by the halting of low-priority trains in the loops to give precedence to faster trains. The only building on the visible section of the layout was the signal box! Personally, I think that, if you have the space, this type of layout has much to recommend it. It certainly keeps the viewers' interest at exhibitions. A more up-to-date example of this sort of layout is 'Holiday Haunts', a superb O-gauge layout that has appeared at many shows over recent years.

My second example taken from an exhibition programme is an industrial layout called 'Allied Marine and Locomotive Company'. It was built by Alan Sibley, again

who has ever visited the USA or read about layouts built in that country will know that our American fellow modellers usually build large layouts. What was totally new to me was Tony Koester's concept of 'Building Blocks', or 'Layout Design Elements' as he calls them. He calls it 'prototype plagiarism' and says that we should 'think of it as a connect-the-dots or jigsaw puzzle approach to layout design'. Each 'building block' (LDE) is simply a copy of key elements of a specific prototype track arrangement. On that basis he says 'we can be reasonably sure that our model railroad will look realistic and operate plausibly. Stringing several LDEs together completes the picture.' In his book he looks at areas such as 'Towns and Cities', 'Junctions', 'Industries', 'Small and mid-size yards' and 'Engine terminals'.

While the terminology 'Layout Design Element' is new to me, it is in effect what I am suggesting in this book, although most of us do not have space to 'string the elements together to make a large layout'. Nevertheless, the idea

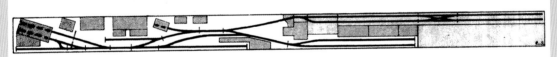

Plan of 'Allied Marine and Locomotive Company'

– if I remember rightly – in the late 1970s. It was an OO-gauge layout measuring 12 feet by 1 foot depicting a fictitious but typical engineering works and its internal railway system. It demonstrated very well Alan's view that industrial modelling provides much more interesting operation than the conventional branch-line terminus to fiddle yard layout often seen in a 12 feet by 1 foot area.

Finally, while writing this chapter I came across a book entitled *Realistic Model Railroad Building Blocks* by Tony Koester, published by Kalmbach Books in the USA. Anyone

of modelling a loco shed, a shunting yard, a small terminus, a small dock or whatever, is what most of us are familiar with in the UK.

Tony Koester realises that, even in the USA, homeowners have to use 'selective compression', and says that this should be done by 'reproducing some of the prototype elements, not all of them'. Essentially what he is saying is what is true of railway modellers the world over – 'look to the prototype for inspiration and examples'. If you do that, you should produce a realistic model railway.

2 • Prototype scenic detail

I said in the Introduction that the secret of building a convincing layout is to concentrate on producing something that looks prototypical. This is not in any way to condemn 'tail-chaser layouts' with no scenery – if they give their builders pleasure they have achieved their objective, because the reason for building model railways must surely be that we wish to enjoy doing it. I do not suppose that the builders of such layouts would claim that they were prototypical, since that was never their intention.

My own view is that, if you concentrate on scenic detail, you are well on the way to producing a convincing layout. By scenic detail, I do not necessarily mean concentrating on every tiny detail, although that can be fascinating – I am referring to the wider picture. For example, if you are modelling a terminus or a through station, nearby there may be any of the following: a bus depot; a coach depot; a haulage contractor's depot; a second-hand car lot with a portable

building for an office; a refuse vehicle depot; a car dealership/garage; or a railway engineering depot. All these provide the opportunity to use many of the vehicles produced commercially at very reasonable prices in many scales. Not only that, Bachmann produces various models of buildings in its Scenecraft range that can be incorporated. Metcalfe also produces a bus

The delightful clutter of a trackside scrapyard. *Author*

depot in 4mm scale, which could be used – and not just as a bus depot. The railway engineering depot would provide the opportunity to use the yellow-painted road vehicles that go with such a location.

If you want to model more open spaces but wish to include vehicles, you could model a vintage vehicle rally, which is a very common sight, especially near preserved railways. Other possibilities for an open space are a caravan rally or, for example, a Land Rover rally, as again suitable models are available.

If you are modelling an urban or built-up area, it is quite common to find a scrapyard near the railway line. This can be an opportunity to use old damaged models of cars stacked high together with other suitable scrap; models not in a good condition can be picked up very cheaply at toy fairs and some exhibitions. My son Justin built a model of a scrapyard on his layout when he was a teenager (see picture opposite). Also, certain scrapyards concentrate on 'white goods' – 'Widnes Vine Yard' layout has such a feature, as shown in the July 2011 issue of *British Railway Modelling*.

Yet another possibility is an MOT testing station for HGV vehicles. The possibilities are endless if you keep your eyes open. If you can take photographs, so much the better, but please remember to ask. It is only polite to explain why you want to do it, and in my experience you will almost always receive ready cooperation.

In the Introduction I mentioned 'The Buckingham Branch' built by the late Rev Peter Denny. This was a classic model railway, but the whole thing was an imaginary branch line as it might have been seen in 1907. What gave it its authenticity was that it was very realistically operated and the buildings – railway and non-railway – were scale models taken from various places, for example a gas works based on Truro, a chapel and timber-framed house from examples at Northleach, a goods shed based on that at Burnley, and an overall roof covering the platform from Chester Northgate. Yet, when put together, a very convincing overall picture resulted.

Buildings are one of the most important items. Accessories also make the model railway come alive. Whether they are telegraph poles, lamp posts, coal pens or luggage barrows on platforms, they are all important in achieving the overall effect we are seeking to produce.

Figures also are important, in my opinion, although I have to say that some modellers would disagree because they do not like miniature people in 'frozen positions'. But there are many good figures on the market in most popular gauges, and I think they also add to the impression we are trying to produce.

Another superb layout, of which I have personal experience, was the late John Pomroy's 'Winton', an LNER layout in 4mm scale. It portrayed an imaginary station in the 1930s and was so successfully done that viewers used to say things like 'it must be in Yorkshire or somewhere near'. John did this by copying actual structures from the area concerned. 'Winton' was initially built as a terminus. It had double track and the operating potential was enhanced by providing a small yard and a single-line branch to a small port, which generated traffic to and from the main line. There was only room for John to model a small country station if he was to create the illusion of space that railways often have. When he built the layout, he had three aims:

- To create a station on a double-track main line, providing interesting operation with good-length trains
- To attempt to capture the LNER atmosphere of the 1930s
- To build a portable layout with reliable operation

The fact that the crowd in front of the layout at exhibitions was frequently three or four deep showed how well John succeeded in achieving those aims, particularly the third one.

Planning such a layout takes time. For example, at an early stage John measured all his locos and rolling stock. These measurements were then used to determine the lengths of sidings, loops and clearances for running round, as well as the length of the roads in the fiddle yard. The LNER atmosphere came from

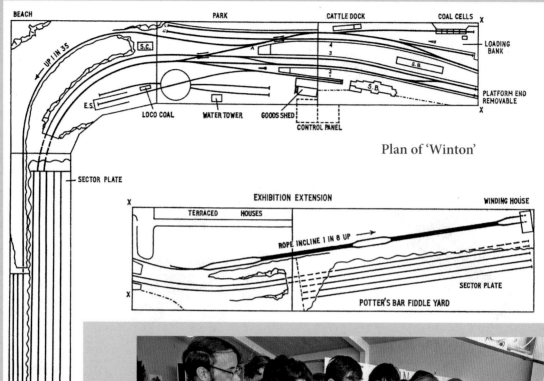

Plan of 'Winton'

As can be seen, in operation 'Winton' was very popular. A much younger author is seen near the children, trying to push the barrier back! *Coventry Evening Telegraph*

the buildings and, of course, the locomotives and rolling stock used.

I had a small involvement with this layout in that I had the privilege of being one of the operators at many exhibitions in the 1970s. John took realism into a different realm by having a sequence timetable of ten different trains from end to end of the layout and back again, plus trains on the branch line. The sequence was accompanied by a tape recording describing the trains and various features of the layout. It started as follows:

'And so we ask you to imagine a cool summer morning about 35 years ago, a sea fret hangs over the cliffs, a tinkle of bells is heard from the box, a signal is raised and the early morning newspaper and mail train approaches from York...'

If you want to read John's own account of 'Winton', look for a copy of the November 1972

Railway Modeller in which it was 'Railway of the Month'. I picked up a copy at the South Devon Railway recently for 10p.

After a short time, fellow members of the Oxford MRC built a 10-foot extension to turn 'Winton' into a through station at exhibitions. This added a great deal of interest both for operators and spectators.

While mentioning timetables, these can be another reason for building a layout. If operating is your interest, why not build a layout precisely because you want to operate it to a timetable you have compiled? The timetable can be put together in a number of different ways. It can be a simple sequence of moves or it can be much more complicated – it can also be run to a speeded-up clock. The choice is yours.

The late Cyril Freezer, when Editor of *Railway Modeller*, once said that he thought that the ultimate in timetable operation was carried out on 'The Sherwood Section of the LMS'. It was highly complex and included every conceivable working that one could possibly imagine on the prototype railway. The builder of the layout (the late Norman Eagles) was, at the peak of his career, as Schedules Superintendent for the London Transport bus system. Another thing that set 'The Sherwood Section' apart from other layouts was that the locomotives were all clockwork. Having had the privilege of seeing the layout in the flesh in the large room in Norman's garden and having been allowed to operate it under instruction, I can vouch for the fact that it was absolutely fascinating. The fact that the scenery was rudimentary in no way took away the enjoyment and fulfilment of operating it.

When the layout movements started the time was taken as being 4am at Sherwood. When the operating session finished the time was noted and the next session would start at that time, and so on. It took about four sessions to complete the 24-hour timetable, so operating did not become boring, and there were six operating positions. In the case of delays, the Controller decided what trains should be held and for how long and if any movements should be cancelled or modified. This system may not suit everyone but it is a valid way of modelling

if that is your particular interest.

Another common lineside industry was a woodyard or a timber merchant; even today there is one near Welshpool station, though the old station building is now owned by Edinburgh Woollen Mills and a bypass now separates the timber merchant from the railway line and the new 'basic' station.

Some years ago my son Justin built an OO-gauge layout called 'Mullacombe'. As I had done on one of my layouts, he had the name sign for exhibitions professionally produced. It was so good that he chose to call his latest layout by the same name, so that is 'Mullacombe (Mk 2)'. When he was building the original 'Mullacombe' we were at an exhibition and he spotted a group of timberyard buildings for sale on a second-hand stall. They were reasonably priced so he bought them and incorporated them into his layout. When he moved into his own home in 2001 the layout would not fit, so he scrapped it and built his current layout, but retained the timberyard buildings for future use.

Imagine our surprise when at an exhibition not all that many years ago I was looking through the old magazines for sale only to find a copy of the June 1964 issue of *Model Railway News* that included an article entitled 'A Wayside Woodyard' describing the buildings that Justin had bought. They were built by Maurice Kelly and there was a set of drawings, which I have taken the liberty of reproducing here – sadly *Model Railway News* has long since ceased production. I think Maurice Kelly was an operator on Norman Eagles's layout 'The Sherwood Section of the LMS', so I may have met him when I visited that layout in the 1970s with members of the Oxford MRC. The railway modelling fraternity is a small world. I believe Maurice Kelly has since died, but if I am wrong and he reads this, 'Thank you, Maurice' – the buildings are in good hands.

When visiting Justin in 2011 while this book was being written, we got out the timberyard buildings and photographed them on his dining table. I think that they look very good still and are now at least 48 years old, or possibly older. They are a tribute to Maurice Kelly's modelling skills and I am sure they will appear on one of Justin's layouts in the future. They were not an exact copy of an actual woodyard but were broadly based on a site local to where Maurice Kelly lived.

The photographs of various scenic details in this chapter will, I hope, give the reader inspiration. It is not intended that they be copied slavishly but rather that they should serve as 'thought provokers' or ideas that can be the catalyst for an instantly recognisable scene on your layout.

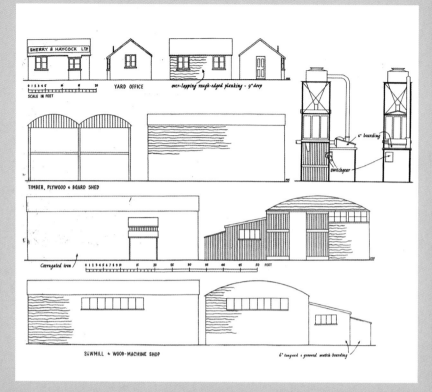

Drawings of Maurice Kelly's 'Wayside Woodyard', and photographs of the buildings by the author.

An elderly Fowler shunter at Kingsbury scrapyard on 8 May 1981. Notice the state of the loco and rolling stock, the yard surface and the scrap lying around – a general picture of dirt and dereliction! *Ray Ruffell*

A Hunslet shunter on shed at Baddesley Colliery on 9 September 1982. *Ray Ruffell*

Another Hunslet, this time a 2-foot-gauge 0-6-0 on the surface railway at Whittle Colliery on 16 July 1981. Again, note the state of the surface and the wire fence. *Ray Ruffell*

I just had to include these photographs because I started my 28-year career in the motor industry at Pressed Steel Co at Cowley (Oxford) in April 1958. The Swindon factory was opened in 1955, and in 1966 Pressed Steel merged with BMC to form British Motor Holdings. In 1968 BMH and Leyland merged to form British Leyland, the car division being known as BL Cars. I started my career as an Estimator, but in 1969 I moved into Purchasing and in 1971 negotiated the contract with British Rail to ship Allegro pressings from Swindon to Longbridge, which already had an extensive internal rail system. Eventually I became Traffic Co-ordination Manager for BL Cars working closely with the Facilities Planning Department to rationalise the traffic flows between the major plants. BL Cars also had a factory in Seneffe in Belgium, and we looked at various traffic movements between the UK and Belgium using roll-on roll-off ferries.

The first picture shows the Pressed Steel Swindon factory's 0-4-0 Fowler diesel on 6 February 1981. The building behind it would make a good model. The factory is now owned by BMW and is a shadow of what it was in its heyday when it had two toolrooms, a pattern shop, three press shops and three body-in-white assembly buildings. *Ray Ruffell*

Middle: In this view of Longbridge on 15 February 1984 the signal box is under the conveyor joining two parts of the huge site. The overbridge and station are in the background, and the 0-4-0 Longbridge factory diesel loco is stabled by the loco shed. *Ray Ruffell*

Bottom: The Cofton Hackett factory at Longbridge produced engines. On the same day one of the Longbridge diesels is shunting a 16T mineral wagon. The buildings in the background would make excellent low-relief buildings if you were modelling a factory. Note the downpipes, the pipe on a 'stretcher wire' and the security lights. The latter can be easily added to your layout and be made to work. *Ray Ruffell*

This is the Blue Circle Cement factory at Plymstock on 24 March 1981, with a diesel-hydraulic loco pulling a train of cement wagons out of the building. Again, the building could be easily modelled using corrugated sheet plasticard. Nigel Bowyer did this very effectively for the buildings on his 'Napier Street' 7mm layout; in fact, he used Wills 4mm corrugated sheeting, but it did not look out of place. Notice too the skip – easily available and very prototypical. *Ray Ruffell*

An 0-4-0 diesel shunts at C. C. Crump's wagon works at Connah's Quay on 16 February 1984. A wagon works is another good modelling possibility. There are many wagons and vans available in the popular scales and many suitable kits that can be 'kit-bashed' or used 'out of the box' to make the works. Low-relief buildings for the backscene would very much add to the overall picture. *Ray Ruffell*

Below: I could not resist including this photograph! It was taken on 27 June 1983 at the Darlington Chemical & Insulating ('Darchem') factory, and shows part of the internal rail system,

which used Ruston diesels. The state of the track, the lack of ballast and the buildings make it superbly atmospheric! *Ray Ruffell*

Below: At ICI's Runcorn factory on 13 December 1983 Yorkshire 0-6-0 diesel *R. A. Lawday* is at the head of the train of tanker wagons. This would make an excellent subject for a model railway if you have space. The Knightwing 'pipework kit' in OO gauge would be particularly useful here. *Ray Ruffell*

Electro-diesel No E6103 backs into 39 Berth at Southampton Eastern Docks for the second 'Northern Star' boat train to Waterloo. There is a wealth of detail here, and what an opportunity to include a large car park on your layout utilising many of the vehicles available to modellers today in the popular scales. The only drawback is the amount of space required! *Ray Ruffell*

If space is limited, how about something like this? This is Painters engineering works in Hereford on 11 March 1983. Such an establishment would be ideal for a small layout, with the entrance to the building in the background giving access to the cassette area or fiddle yard. *Ray Ruffell*

Another possibility for a model is one of the Armed Forces Depots. This photograph was taken at RAF Chilmark on 16 June 1981. *Ray Ruffell*

Three shed scenes: in the first two 'Q1' 0-6-0s are having their smokeboxes cleaned at Guildford shed on 16 May 1965. The 'clutter' is easily modelled – note that the sleepers are totally buried. *Ray Ruffell*

Bolton shed on 23 March 1968. Again there is so much detail to take in, from the coaling tower down to the yard lamps and sleepers lying between the tracks. *Ray Ruffell*

A Class 37 diesel stands at Margam diesel depot on 24 April 1975. Note the clock, the 'Stop & Proceed with Caution' sign, the numbers '1' and '2' above the two roads into the shed, the lights on the front of the shed, and the oil drums lying around haphazardly on the right. *Ray Ruffell*

Above: This photograph of Paignton station, taken on 24 April 1982, shows the 17.25 service to Paddington leaving. I think this scene has tremendous possibilities, allowing you to model the modern era alongside a preserved railway, in this case the Paignton & Dartmouth Steam Railway, which is on the left of the photograph. You have a ready-made use for some of the excellent vehicles available to modellers these days. *Ray Ruffell*

Below: This is Bridgnorth shed on the Severn Valley Railway on 6 October 1984. The location of the shed next to the platform has distinct modelling possibilities. Notice the enthusiasts all over the yard and on the footbridge. *Ray Ruffell*

Examples of 'clutter' in Pendre Yard on the Talyllyn Railway and at Buckfastleigh on the South Devon Railway. Note also other features such as the puddles, the surface of the yard and, in some places, how the weeds have grown around the 'clutter'. I personally love adding this sort of detail as I think it really adds authenticity to the layout. *All author*

Top and middle: **More clutter!** The first two photographs were taken on the quay at Bangor (North Wales) where the Penrhyn Quarry line terminated when the slates were brought down from the quarry for transhipment to the ships. I believe these buildings were originally owned by the quarry, but they are now used by local businesses. Nevertheless, the detail is there – for example, the boarded-up windows, rust on the doors, and miscellaneous items stacked outside the building. *Both Author*

Bottom: The third picture was taken on the Dart Valley Railway, and again the detail is marvellous. Corrugated buildings, buffers, a skip, a boiler, a loco cab, weeds growing up the fence, tarpaulin-covered items, a flimsy chain-link fence, and puddles on a rough surface. You could spend hours recreating a scene like this and it could be done easily and cheaply, using bits out of the scrap box. *Author*

Note again the ground surface. This photograph, taken at the Llangollen Railway, shows the advantage of modelling a preserved railway (real or imagined) as you can justifiably have steam and diesel locos of all shapes and sizes next to one another in the engine shed area. *Author*

A new water tank, the old one on the floor, a point lever and the ground surface are all worthy of note here. The photograph was taken at the terminus of the Bala Lake Railway at Llanuwchllyn near Bala. *Author*

The shed at Churston on the Paignton & Dartmouth Railway presents a tidier scene. Note the black and yellow stripes on the door, the modern buildings, the 'ladder on wheels' and the various shades of the 'hardstanding'. *Author*

There are many vehicles available to modellers in the popular scales. If, like me, you like vintage vehicles, one way of justifying the use of a wide range of them is to model a vintage vehicle rally, as here on the South Devon Railway. The photographs show that it is possible to have a very wide selection of vehicles on your layout. You can even make 'signs' like the one propped in front of the Riley JFM 446. *Both author*

The bus standing outside the station at Buckfastleigh is being used to transport passengers to and from Buckfast Abbey. The use of the vintage bus means that it is not incongruous to have modern vehicles alongside it. *Author*

This picture of Douglas shed on the Isle of Man is superb for scenic detail enthusiasts like me! The Scammell Scarab, with the loco boiler on the trailer, the wheel sets in the foreground, the buildings and the carriage all combine to make a very atmospheric scene that could be easily modelled.
David Mitchell

Inside the engine shed at the Bala Lake Railway. There is a wealth of detail here – look at all the lamps stored on the left.
Author

Finally, there's a prototype for everything! This view of the Vale of Rheidol station at Aberystwyth, taken some years ago, shows that if you were short of space your run-round loop could cross the platform!
Author

3 · Realistic model scenic detail

In 1982 *Model Railways* magazine (no longer in existence) published an 'extra' entitled 'Compact Model Railways'. It was written by the late Cyril Freezer, who was then editor of that magazine. In the chapter entitled 'The Importance of Detail' he wrote the following:

'For the majority, the question of detail is not so much making an exact replica of the original, but reproducing the essence of the prototype… But it takes time and a load of observations of the prototype.'

This perfectly sums up my thoughts on the subject of model scenic detail.

I said in the Introduction that, in my opinion, the secret of building a convincing layout is to produce something that looks prototypical and realistic. Therefore it follows that photographs of the prototype are a huge help, which is why I included so many of various prototype aspects in the previous chapter.

As we saw with John Pomroy's 'Winton' layout, buildings are one of the most important items. People looking at his layout immediately recognised that it was a portrayal of somewhere in Yorkshire because of the buildings and the materials used. For example, I live in mid-Wales and the slate-mining industry was tremendously important here for many years; it is therefore not surprising that the older cottages and houses have Welsh slate roofs.

You do not have to construct your buildings from scratch if you prefer not to. There are many good kits available, in both plastic and card, and there are also ready-made buildings available. For example, Bachmann produces a bus depot, an office block, a lineside transformer site, fuel storage tanks, low relief shops, and a low-relief bonded warehouse, to mention only a few, while in the Hornby range there is a modern factory front, a pub, workshops, a GWR engine shed, a model of Radley signal box, a water column and crane, and a modern-traction engine shed. These examples are all for OO gauge, but there are similar buildings also available in N and O gauge.

Earlier I mentioned books written by Peter Denny and P. D. Hancock about their layouts. Silver Link Publishing produced John Parkinson's book *Creative Scenic Modelling*, which again I can recommend as being very helpful. You will also see John and his layout regularly on the exhibition circuit.

My interest in scenic detail started when I built a small 009 motive power depot in 1972, which is described more fully on pages 63 to 65 of *Layouts for Limited Spaces*, first published in 1996 by Silver Link Publishing and still available through them or in bookshops. It was built on a baseboard that measured only 35 inches by 21 inches, yet I was able to include all the 'clutter' and more than 100 figures and it still did not look overcrowded. The layout won a number of awards at exhibitions for best scenic detail.

When I changed scales and moved into modelling in 7mm narrow gauge (often referred to as 0-16.5) I built another motive power depot, which is also more fully described in *Layouts for Limited Spaces*. As can be seen from the photograph on page 42, with the use of a traverser it is very easy to get a layout such as this into a relatively small space – in this case 80 by 16 inches on two boards, each 40 inches long – and still include a lot of scenic detail. Also, using easily available materials such as the Airfix water tower kit, balsa wood, scrap wheel sets, etc, it is easy to produce a convincing picture. The fact that the Airfix kit is meant for OO gauge does not matter, and it looks right in my opinion.

Let us now look at a selection of photographs

The author's 009 motive power depot layout of 1972. *Both B. Higgins*

of sections of layouts that portray convincing scenes/cameos taken from the prototype. The last, on pages 42 and 43, have been provided by Gordon Gravett — study them well as they are marvellous examples of what I am trying to say about the importance of scenic detail on a layout. Gordon has also written

two books entitled *7mm Modelling*. Part 1 is 'An Introduction' and Part 2 is 'Building a Layout', and both are published by Wild Swan Publications Ltd. They are well worth a read, and not just for those who model in 7mm scale. I continually refer to my copies.

My 7mm narrow gauge shed layout featured a traverser, a great space-saver! *Author*

Middle and bottom: The current exhibition layout built by Gordon Gravett and his wife Maggie, 'Pempoul Reseau Breton', is absolutely stunning and is based on the metre-gauge system that once served inland Brittany connecting rural villages and towns with the SNCF main lines. The layout depicts a fictitious small section of the railway in the last years of its life, together with a taste of the area through which it ran. It is all scratch-built to a scale of 1:50 and, if it is ever at an exhibition near you, make the effort to go and see it. You will not be disappointed. *All Gordon Gravett*

The other three photographs provided by Gordon are two of the diorama of the winding house above Abergynolwyn on the Talyllyn Railway, and one of 'Ditchling Green', which was a superb O-gauge layout that Gordon and Maggie built and exhibited at many shows some years ago; it is 0-16.5 gauge (i.e. 7mm narrow gauge). The original winding house has long since disappeared, but the diorama shows what it used to be like. It was donated to the Talyllyn Railway by Gordon and Maggie and can be seen in the TR shop. *All Gordon Gravett*

This is Keith Wright's layout 'Cripple Corner'. The track plan and another photograph appears on page 31 of my book *More Layouts for Limited Spaces*, and I make no apology for using more photographs of it here as these photographs just 'ooze' atmosphere. The layout depicts a wagon repair works in an industrialised area of the North East of England. *All Tony Wright, courtesy of BRM*

These photographs of the Yeovil Model Railway Group's 'Gas Works' layout (see also the title page and page 64) have been selected not because they identify scenes from a gasworks, but because the scenes they portray so beautifully could be incorporated into any number of layouts. The first shows a platform backed by a retaining wall, with various loads waiting to be moved; the lighting really adds to the overall scene. The second shows a superb factory building, made from corrugated sheeting that is going rusty, served by a wagon turntable; the foreground could be on any dockside, river or canal layout. Finally, the third view shows various items of scenic detail – the young lad looking through the fence, the fence itself, the superb buildings and the overgrown path. Perhaps above all, the various different levels really add to the overall picture that your eyes take in as you look at the model. *All Bob Alderman*

These three photographs show scenes from Derek Gelsthorpe's 'Idle Way' layout. The first shows the railway alongside the canal boat with a factory behind the realistic fence. The very realistic backscene in the second picture really adds depth to the layout, while the third shows the simple refuelling point and associated clutter; note the 'feeder pipe' coming from the building. *All author*

Above: **Here is a very simple but effective small scenic feature. Camping sites are quite common alongside railway lines, especially in Mid-Wales where I live. This one shows cars and caravans in the same field as the Scout Camp. I presume the 'garden shed' acts as the camp site office.** *Author*

Below: **Another simple but effective lineside feature: this time the train is passing a beach, as it still does at Dawlish, for example, today. This scene is on the Redditch MRC's exhibition layout 'Dagnall End'.** *Author*

This scene on my Gn15 layout 'Iron Street Sheds' shows, I believe, how a layout can be 'brought to life' by the addition of figures and simple scenic details such as the signs on the building in the background. I particularly like the two figures (Bachmann) near the hoist looking at a drawing or plan; they are portrayed as 'doing something' but are not in unrealistic poses. *Author*

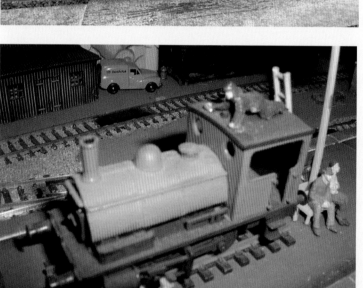

My elder son Justin got the idea of putting a small loco on the platform of his 'Mullacombe' layout from a photograph he saw of *Shannon* on the platform at Wantage Road station. He has taken the idea a stage further by having men working on the loco to finally make it look presentable in its finished state. *Author*

A superb derelict building on Mike Bragg's 'Lenches Bridge' layout. This is still a common scene on many lines today, for example when approaching Wolverhampton from Shrewsbury and between Wolverhampton and Birmingham. *Author*

A scene on the author's layout 'The Shed' – two ladies talking by the back gate, a man sawing wood, the small car parked between the back wall of the terraced homes, and the container stored in the yard. The tracks on the layout run behind the scenic detail at the front, thus giving something for the viewer to 'look through', which is what generally happens in real life unless the viewer is actually at the lineside. *Author*

The first of these two photographs of the author's 'Stabling Point' layout (see page 121) gives the overall impression of such a scene that our eyes take in when we look at the prototype or model. *Author*

Some of the detail that goes to 'make up the whole': the tank, the lean-to office building, the skip, the clutter and the locos. *Author*

Above: A scene full of various 'cameos' on Kevin Cartwright's 'Stodmarsh' layout, which together give a marvellous overall picture. *Craig Tiley, courtesy of Model Rail*

Right: A more specific close-up depiction of the smithy at work – note again the detail. *Craig Tiley, courtesy of Model Rail*

These two scenes from 'Teesside Steel' are full of 'cameos' that make up a superb whole. Where the new pipes are being laid, note the planks in place to prevent the trench collapsing. *Both Jeff Wetherall*

The first of these two views of 'George Street Stabling Point' by Mark Murray (see page 81) shows the 'business' of the scene, the clutter, the van, the fork-lift truck and the building, all 'framed', as it were, by the retaining wall and the fence above it. It all combines to make a very convincing overall picture. The other photograph shows a 'cameo' at the entrance to the stabling point, with a loco passing a permanent way gang at work. The factory building acts as a very good background to this very convincing picture – convincing because it portrays so well the real thing, seen regularly on our railways. *Both Mark Murray*

'Tolcarn Engine Shed', built by Terry Yeend of Wolverhampton, was a marvellous layout and was widely exhibited both in the UK and in Europe. These very atmospheric views have that magic 'something' that makes you think it is the real thing. *Both Tony Wright, courtesy of British Railway Modelling*

The 'Haslington TMD' layout was built by Stan Bennett and two friends. Note the car parking bays marked out – easily done but not seen very often – and the terraced housing behind the typical wire mesh fence, creating a convincing overall scene. *Both Stan Bennett*

'Howards Bank' was another layout built by Stan Bennett and his friends. I particularly like the two levels seen in the first picture; in the other there are two levels again, but this time emphasised by the road bridge crossing the tracks and the Portakabins stacked one above the other. *Both Stan Bennett*

'George Street Stabling Point Mk 1' was built by Richard Scott (see page 79). Again there are two levels, even if the higher one is only depicted by the backscene above the retaining wall and the fence, but it adds depth to the overall picture in a very small area. Note also the 'clutter' and the fork-lift truck. *Both Richard Scott*

These three very convincing photographs show 'Bank Hall Sidings'. Note in the first the overgrown land this side of the wagons. In the second there's plenty of detail in the back garden and the hoarding on the end wall, while the third view shows the water tank and retaining wall above a particularly convincing portrayal of 'standing' water. *All Derek Shore*

A scene from 'Seahouses' that is not often modelled – boats in a harbour when the tide is out. This is superbly done by Kevin Cartwright and is extremely realistic. *Tony Wright, courtesy of British Railway Modelling*

This is an excellent example of what might be called 'non-railway detail'. It is a view of one of the cottages on Ian Drummond's 'Waterhulme' layout and portrays a very convincing scene of the conservatory on the back of the cottage, the garden seat, the swing and the children playing in the garden – another scene so often seen in real life but not very often modelled, and certainly not as convincingly as Ian has done. The cottage was built from a PME Studios kit to which Ian added extra detailing. *Ian Drummond*

This page: These four superb photographs show Jack Burnard's 'North Hetton Colliery' layout (see page 71). The first demonstrates how convincing it can be to 'dim the lights' over an exhibition layout and portray a dusk or night scene. The second view (left) is included simply to show the internal detail of the small hut! *Both Steve Flint, courtesy of Railway Modeller*

Above right: This photograph shows the working conveyor and the nearby buildings. I particularly like the high-level building with the man coming out of the door and the men working on the platform below. *Steve Flint, courtesy of Railway Modeller*

Right: Very convincing 'non-railway' scenes like this add so much to the overall picture and make the viewer believe it is real. Note particularly the drains and manhole covers in the road, the parked cars and scooter, the telegraph poles *and* wires, and the man opening the door to go into the little shop. *Steve Flint, courtesy of Railway Modeller*

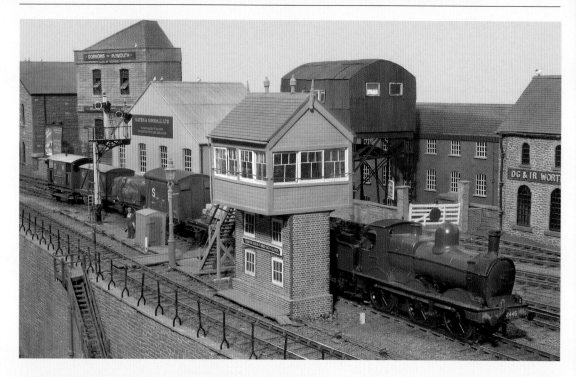

Finally we have three photographs of 'Cornwallis Yard', which show how effectively the layout uses different levels – the viewer's eye is drawn naturally from the lower level to the buildings at the back of the upper level. The second photograph is included mainly for the buildings and the effective signage on them. Note also the two seagulls on the roof of the building in the background and the one on the building at the top right of the picture. If you wanted an advert for a layout with good overall scenic detail, surely this would be it. The picture as a whole is extremely convincing and realistic. Note in the third photograph the overall detail, but particularly the three drain pipes, the signal on its cantilevered platform and the very effective overlapping of the corrugated sheets on the black building in the background. *All Steve Flint, courtesy of Railway Modeller*

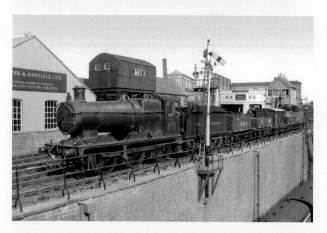

82G (O gauge) described by Nigel Smith

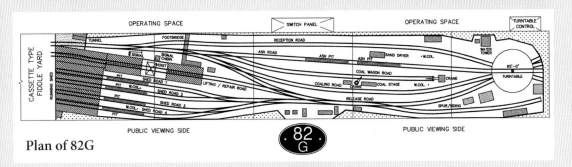

Plan of 82G

Back in 2001, after almost 10 years on the exhibition circuit with the famous 'Loco Clinic', it was decided that we needed something on which to exhibit and run our completed locomotives, set against a 'real' backdrop. Being predominantly locomotive modellers, what better than a loco shed layout?

We wanted a location that would realistically accept locos of the former Great Western, LMS and Southern companies, and the area around Bristol seemed to fit the bill perfectly. Old 'Ian Allans' were consulted and the next available shed code was chosen from the Bristol District of the Western Region (excepting, of course, the later redesignation of former SR sheds taken over by the WR). Rather than trying to think up a fictitious name for the shed, we decided it would

be nice and somewhat different to stick with the shed code as its title – and so '82G' was born.

The track layout is an adaptation of that found at Bournemouth (SR), with the layout being heavily 'Westernised' but still retaining

An excellent photograph looking towards the shed, showing the pits and the water crane with its associated brazier to stop the water from freezing. *Tony Wright, courtesy of British Railway Modelling*

Another marvellous photograph, this time of the shed interior – something not very often modelled. Again, it is so realistic! *Tony Wright, courtesy of British Railway Modelling*

a few 'Southern' touches. The famous lifting shed and hoist from Bournemouth have been deliberately 'retained' and really do make an impressive sight.

Our modelling interests centre on former Great Western, Southern and LMS steam between nationalisation and the mid-1950s, hence the preponderance of motive power in the standard BR liveries. However, you will notice that we also like to throw in a few of the more quirky liveries. The early years of BR were very interesting, as many locos still carried their pre-nationalisation liveries, either with their original numbers and 'branding' or renumbered with 'British Railways' spelled out on the tenders or tank sides. You will see a number of these on

shed at '82G'. You may even see some of the early BR experimental liveries carried by one or two locos.

But it is not all BR steam by any means. We have one or two locos running from an earlier era, mainly for their uniqueness or novelty

A view from above looking across the yard. *Tony Wright, courtesy of British Railway Modelling*

value. A case in point is GWR No 111 *The Great Bear* in all her 1920s glory. We have also started rolling out a few 'Westerns', 'Warships', 08 diesel shunters, 'Hymeks' and 'Brush' Type 4s. So, steam doesn't get all its own way.

We can easily muster 50-60 locomotives for an exhibition, and this build-up of stock is starting to make for some really nice operating scenarios. We can operate with a blend of Western, Southern and Midland Region steam, or run the shed as 'Western' or 'Southern' only. We have also started the day with the 'usual' steam mix, gradually introducing the diesels while slowly removing the older steam classes, until only the diesels remain, with a smattering of those steam classes that lasted to the end of steam. The audience seem to appreciate these variations and this is definitely something we will work on for the future.

About 10 years after the first idea, '82G' is just about finished, even if every time we meet up we seem to find another two or three jobs to do. The old adage that a layout is never finished is true – if it ever was, we would be searching for something new to do.

The keen-eyed observer, seeing the layout at exhibitions will notice that the whole scene

This final view of '82G' speaks for itself. I showed these photographs to two fellow volunteers on the Talyllyn Railway and they thought they were looking at the 'real thing'. When I said they were pictures of a model, they took some convincing! That says it all. *Tony Wright, courtesy of British Railway Modelling*

is being captured on film by a young Ivo Peters (yes, he did have hair in the 1950s), who just happens to be visiting, capturing for posterity the everyday workings of '82G' for future generations to enjoy. What would Ivo's classic car be worth today, I wonder? The blue Bentley can be seen parked by the small buildings at the front of the layout.

'82G' is only likely to have three or four exhibition outings per year, with the 'Loco Clinic' still continuing to appear at most Gauge O Guild and Larger Scale exhibitions.

We hope you enjoy doing a bit of shed bashing at '82G'. Don't forget your Ian Allan spotter's book, but do keep an eye open for the shed foreman!

Gas Works (O gauge) described by Bob Alderman

Plan of 'Gas Works'

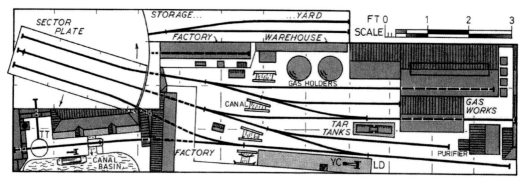

The layout has its origins in the *Model Railway Journal* layout 'Inkerman Street'. The Yeovil Model Railway Group had visited the MRJ exhibition in Central Hall where this layout was exhibited, and the general comment following this was 'very nice but it doesn't do anything'. It also coincided with thoughts that perhaps we should also build a 7mm layout.

The subsequent discussions came up with idea of modelling, at least in part, a gas works. Such industry has at least plenty of traffic – coal in, coke out and various by-products. We would have a layout that had reason for its traffic.

Some tentative track plans were sketched, then 'worked up' into a feasible plan on the CAD system of the company where I worked (lunch times!). The use of a sector plate to store trains and access to the fiddle yard by kick-back saved several points and shortened the layout considerably. Once we thought we had a workable layout we made a model of the model, which enabled ideas of the structures to be applied. It was clear from this that to make the scene work the railway would be dominated by its surrounding buildings – an urban backwater. This led to the decision that

An overall view of 'Gas Works' taken in the Yeovil MRG clubroom. *Bob Alderman*

A view of the fiddle yard.
Bob Alderman

the whole scene would be enclosed, framed like a stage, a proscenium arch to carry the lighting and a covering of 'sky'. The sector plate would be hidden by a secondary similar scene. There is a distinct joint between the two scenes and the differences between the two are such that the inch or two that separates them can be considered to be a couple of miles.

It was from this that splitting the track levels evolved. The run up into the works was obvious, but we felt it could be accentuated if the track next to it dropped into the works. Similarly, obscuring part of the layout by the front rising to the

building over the tracks would be an artifice to *make* the observer look at the railway. In doing this, three typical trainspotting viewpoints were created: looking down through a fence, looking up from the canal, and peering through a doorway.

Several full-size prints of the plan were made. The advantage of using the work CAD was that each of these prints – for baseboard construction, building footprints and trackbuilding – was on one piece of paper. The accuracy was more than good enough for them to be used as templates for point construction. This was in an era before Templot and other planning programmes.

The control panel is at the front of the layout – I am increasingly drawn to operating from the front. Not only is it easier at home, because you can see the whole layout (this is especially true in my shed), but it also means that you can have better contact with the public at exhibitions, and they can also see how the layout is operated, rather than it being 'something that happens out of sight'.
Bob Alderman

The baseboards were made from birch ply following a similar method to that advocated by Barry Norman. Allowances were made for the 'sky' and the first version of this was, frankly, a disaster. It was a quadrant made like an aircraft structure, only with the stringers and frames on the outside of the skin. It was unwieldy and took up a lot of space. This was soon revised to the cloth 'sky' now used.

The trackwork was made from C&L components and plain track. The CAD templates used were quite basic – no 'real' track geometry was drawn, they were just straights and curves at a tangent. Construction adjusted this. Once laid, point motors were added. We had – indeed still have – PFM/Fulgarex motors on our EM layout and they have proved very reliable, so these were used. The motor drives a slider and telescopic square brass tubes, which in turn are connected to the tie bars. One of these motors on the point beside the storage tanks must have made hundreds of thousands of movements, as it is the key to working the layout.

The buildings are constructed in a mixture of materials: plasticard, ply and a reworked plastic kit. The latter, two Heljan engine sheds, forms the basis of the gas works. The low-relief buildings are in plasticard while the large wharf and the building over the tunnel mouths have a ply structure overlaid with embossed Howard Scenics brick. Complex details and many of the windows are resin castings.

Only one of the buildings exists in reality – the one with the arched fronts over the tracks. This was spotted in Bristol even before the layout had been considered, and was photographed as being a good prototype to model. The other buildings have a basis in prototypes, and are often bits, interesting bits, noted on buildings around the country. (I have a collection of photos of these features taken around the UK.) Because the buildings have this foundation in reality, even though

As seen from this very realistic view of the yard, all the details of the buildings, the rolling stock and the ground cover combine to produce a superb overall picture. I particularly like the rusty shed in the foreground. *Bob Alderman*

they do not follow a specific structure they are convincing.

Operation is simple. A train is set up in the fiddle yard and, when ready, the operator calls it forward. Of necessity one operator is at the front of the layout – it cannot be seen from the back. The train is brought to a halt and its wagon type noted. Tank wagons go under the storage tanks, others go to the wharf and foundry. This means many movements back and forth, breaking up the train and sorting the wagons to their appropriate destinations. As the layout is so constrained it is not possible to employ three-link couplings – they would be too difficult to use inside the layout, besides obscuring the observers' view. Alex Jackson couplings enable a hands-free operation when uncoupling stock; electro-magnets are strategically placed to enable all necessary operations to take place. Movements are completed by the reversal of the locomotive and brake-van for the train to go off-scene back to the fiddle yard. The present fiddle yard differs from the original; the sector plate now has direct entry to three storage lines.

While all this is happening the second

operator is running trains in and out of the works. Full and empty wagons come and go, and both coal and coke wagons have removable loads. While doing this he is at the beck and call of the front operator to move the sector plate so that locos can run around their trains. An illuminated request board – for example 'front to middle' – and an attention-attracting buzzer help communication between front and back. The aim when the layout is exhibited is that there is always something going on. In terms of frequency of trains this may be unrealistic, but our view is that we are there to entertain, so keep things moving.

Part of the entertainment is derived from other little features. One is the ability to reduce the lighting level. The lighting consists of three sets of bulbs – white, red and blue – each controlled by a dimmer. Dropping the white lights leaves a red sunset; taking the red down

leaves the blue, giving a moonlit appearance. The speed of change in the lighting levels does sometimes suggest that the layout is in the tropics! The reduction in illumination allows the yard and building lights to show. Some small scenes within the buildings then become apparent, for example the manager in his office and line shafting in a factory.

There is a working wagon turntable by the foundry. With care wagons can be left on it, turned and drawn into the foundry. In addition, the two gas holders slowly rise and fall. There are several figures around the layout, generally in static poses – frozen motion is unbelievable.

The layout was first exhibited in an incomplete form in 1993 and has gone on to be widely exhibited around the UK, and once made a trip to Germany. It has surprised the members that it has been so successful, and we hope it continues to please.

Hospital Gates (O gauge) described by Neil Ripley

Plan of 'Hospital Gates'

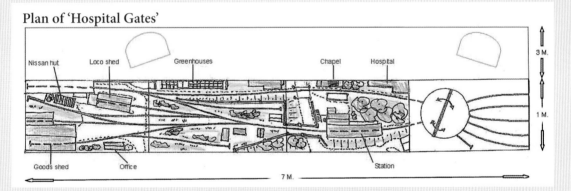

This model, by the East Riding Finescale Group, is envisaged to be elsewhere in the country, but its inspiration is the Lancashire-based Whittingham Hospital Railway. The line opened in 1888, some 20 years after the hospital that it served, forming a connection between the remotely sited grounds and the Longridge branch (LNWR & LYR Joint) at Grimscar. The line was used primarily for conveying the hospital's requirements of stores and fuel. However, platforms were also provided at both ends of the line and a free

passenger service operated for the benefit of staff and visitors. It is recorded that upwards of 400 visitors made use of the service on some Sundays! Steam worked throughout, and the passenger services lasted right up to its 1957 closure.

The line had been worked by a pair of Andrew Barclay 0-4-0T locomotives of 1888 and 1904 vintage respectively, together with a motley collection of ex-North London and LYR four-wheel coaches. However, by the 1940s the system and its stock were life-

This very effective photograph was taken at ground level looking up at the railway. *Steve Flint, courtesy of Railway Modeller*

expired and in serious need of replacement. New passenger stock was effectively created in-house by acquiring and converting a trio of ex-LNWR 20-ton four-wheel goods brakes. Replacement motive power was sourced and purchased second-hand, consisting initially of a former LBSCR 'D1' 0-4-2T, which was joined later by an ex-Bolton Gasworks chain-driven Sentinel!

The layout was strongly influenced by the set-up at the hospital end of the Whittingham system. Its delightful 100-foot-long curved overall-roofed station-cum-carriage shed on an embankment, overbridge, engine shed and goods facility all formed the basis of the inspiration for the structures and general layout that you see on the model. In reality some of the structures have been moved about a bit in relation to each other, and the track layout, although loosely reminiscent of the fan of lines seen in period photographs, is actually of my own design and arranged for its operational potential. However, it has to be said that, somewhat unusually in modelling terms, the area of the prototype on which we have based our model has actually undergone quite a bit of 'selective expansion' in the interests of

better visual and operational potential. The yard trackwork of the prototype is much more compact than we have modelled. Also it had no run-round facility; shunting by way of a rope or by hand using of a BSA petrol-driven wagon-pusher was employed to carry out such manoeuvres. However, the latter were hardly viable options for us, even in 7mm, hence the subtle reworking of the track layout to suit our operational needs.

Following our usual 4mm practice, due thought was given to construction, transportation and storage from the initial design stage. The last two were especially important as the layout's main purpose was for exhibition use, so it needed to be easily transportable and quick to erect and dismantle. As such, the layout consists of four durable baseboards, each having plywood sandwich side-frames, ply tops and integral back/end scenes. These are combined with integral folding legs complete with heavy-duty 'paste-table'-style folding/locking stays. All this ensures that, for all its size, the layout can be erected and dismantled smoothly and in the minimum of time. These are important factors at the end of a weekend's show when you could be facing a journey of many hundreds of miles ahead of you to get home before the day's work is over.

Three of the baseboards – two at 4ft 6in

This lovely view shows the railway, the buildings, the rolling stock and the car. It all adds up to a very realistic and convincing picture. *Steve Flint, courtesy of Railway Modeller*

I particularly like the details just inside the shed, with the two men working at the bench. This photograph really shows what realistic railway modelling is all about – the detail is just right. *Steve Flint, courtesy of Railway Modeller*

and one at 5 feet – are scenic, with the fourth, 5 feet long, forming the fiddle yard at one end. The latter consists of a fan of sidings fed from a train-length turntable, which in turn can feed into the main or Army branch lines. Each board has its own dedicated box cover constructed from thin ply to provide relatively dust-free protection for the vulnerable scenery and track ends, both during transport and storage.

The trackwork and electrics contain no great mystery, as – aside from the interlaced three-way turnout constructed from copper-clad sleepers combined with C&L cosmetic chairs – the model uses durable Peco track throughout, which has been carefully ballasted and weathered and, for much of its length, given a good covering of weeds! Simple to lay, it provided us with both the realistic look we desired and the durability and reliability we required.

Electrics are the black art that is a mystery

Another view from ground level, which gives an excellent picture of the train passing over the bridge, the car coming under it and the man going towards the gate in the distance. *Steve Flint, courtesy of Railway Modeller*

to many modellers, us included! However, we are very fortunate to have an electrician of old among our number, so John Wass was given the task of designing and installing a simple and reliable DCC electrical system, with a separate system for the switch-operated Tortoise point motors and building lighting. Each system was carefully placed, labelled and linked between boards by simple jumper wires with audio plug sockets at the rear.

Simplicity in thinking extends to the fiddle yard turntable. This is powered though a pair of sprung plungers bearing on a brass ring mounted on the underside of the deck. It is fitted with colour indicators and fed through a reversing switch to change the electric polarity on moves where the deck is reversed to the rest of the layout's electrics. Control of all this is capably handled by a durable Bachmann EZ command unit and matching slave, which, given that it is designed for children, makes it an excellent choice for us!

Even though we were never intending to make an accurate model of Whittingham or any other hospital site, they were still extensively researched using period photographs available to us, together with those in books on the area and on the internet. The buildings, including the station, train shed, engine shed and gatehouse all bear strong resemblances to those at Whittingham. However, by virtue of design, construction practicalities and, in some cases, use of available kit parts, none is an exact replica. With the exception of the engine and goods sheds, which make use of plastic kit parts, all of the structures are scratch-built and based on plywood shells with plasticard overlays. In comparison the complex station roof structure (which scales out at 100 feet just like the original) was made from brass, and is the result of many hours of patient work with a soldering iron. It was finished off with Lexan glazing and car pinstripe framing bars for the roof, and laser-cut planking for the sides, both weathered to suit.

The inclusion of a period Nissen hut was in the plans from the start. However, the logistics of its construction (or, to put it another way, it looked difficult to scratch-build and we were putting it off!) fortuitously delayed it long enough for a resin kit to be released by Gramodels, which, as you might imagine, we were more than enthusiastic to use. A couple of grounded bodies created from damaged kit-built vans (Slaters) and a couple of resin huts by Port Wynstay and Unit models completed the structures on the model.

The only other major item was the trees, which were constructed from wire armatures after an evening's master-class for us by Peter Goss of 'Etton' and 'Rowlands Castle' fame. The rest of the ground cover and shrubbery are a heady mix of Woodland Scenics and Javis products, with the in-filled trackwork in the yard area created from paint-tinted grey tile adhesive mixed with PVA. This mix is much easier to work on application and more flexible in subsequent use than plaster. A mixture of white-metal figures, period road vehicles and a hand-painted backscene featuring several structures and scenes from the real Whittingham site bring the scene to life.

In terms of locomotives and rolling stock, the layout fleet differs from its Whittingham inspiration in that our locomotive fleet is larger and certainly more standardised, albeit just as careworn and dog-eared as the prototypes! A trio of Peckett 0-4-0 saddle tanks (ABS and Slaters kits) together with a handful of pensionable ex-company cast-off coaches (Slaters and Pocket Money Kits) form the hospital's fleet.

To reflect the military influence – due to our supposition that a large temporary military hospital and associated railway line to service it has been built in the grounds (as happened at several of these sites) – a military Fowler diesel and requisitioned 'Jazzer' side tank are also on hand to cover the increased traffic flows. Also, at the time of writing a WD Hudswell railcar of the type used on the Spurn Head line is under construction.

The remainder of the rolling stock on the layout was created from kits of Parkside, Slaters and Peco origin. Some of it was built by friends and family who wanted to contribute, and all items are painted and weathered using photos of stock of the period as a guide.

So, has the East Riding Finescale Group's first foray into 7mm scale been a success? Well, from our point of view the answer is yes. The layout and its scenic details have proved popular with viewing audiences and exhibition organisers alike and, despite our limiting the number of shows we can attend per year, it has already made successful long-distance forays south of London and overseas into Europe as well as attending more local events in the north of the country. Many more shows are already planned both here and in Europe to keep us busy for years to come.

So there you have it. The layout you see in the photographs was built over a three-year period by a group of modellers with no previous 7mm modelling experience, no guidance, no guide books, and certainly very little in the way of a clue where to actually start. Still, with experimentation, a whole lot of enthusiasm and finding out that the steep learning curve is all part of the fun, once you get over the scale difference, 7mm modelling proves no more daunting than its 4mm equivalent. All you need is a whole lot more materials and patience (and money!) to do it!

North Hetton Colliery (Gauge 1) described by Jack Burnard

Plan of 'North Hetton Colliery'

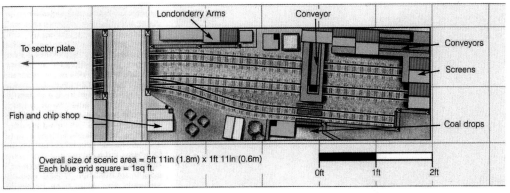

Overall size of scenic area = 5ft 11in (1.8m) x 1ft 11in (0.6m)
Each blue grid square = 1sq ft.

This layout has an overall size of 9 feet by 2 feet, and a viewable area of 6 feet by 2 feet. The scale is 1:32 (approximately 10mm to 1 foot). It is a freelance depiction of a 1950s Durham colliery, representing a very small drift mine that would have been part of a larger colliery complex. The layout was designed to be transported to exhibitions in a small

The three photographs on this spread by Steve Flint are good examples of what this book is about – railway modelling realism. It is hard to believe that they are photographs of a Gauge 1 minimum-space layout. Not only are they very realistic, but they also just 'ooze' atmosphere and details. *Steve Flint, courtesy of Railway Modeller*

hatchback car, and I have since sold it to a friend who also exhibits it at exhibitions.

As most of my previous layouts had also been collieries, named after local pits, I had started to run out of names, so I used a name from a little further away. North Hetton Colliery was the name for a complex of three pits, Moorsley Pit, Hazard Pit and Dunwell Pit. They were part of an independent company that were absorbed by the Lambton, Hetton and Joicey Collieries. The coal obtained from them was transported to the staithes at Sunderland for transport by ship to the south. The original collieries closed in 1935 and I have assumed that they have reopened during the Second World War as a drift mine, as the main source of coal was

quite close to the surface.

The design of the layout took as much time as its construction. My layouts are made for exhibition display only, so have to attract the paying public. This means that something has to be happening most of the time. To overcome this problem, a conveyor that loads coal into mine wagons was used; I had used conveyors previously and they are a positive attraction on any layout.

Using a sector-plate fiddle yard saved space that I could use for a third siding (see the layout plan). This was used as a small coal depot to

provide coal for the local miners. There was just enough space to include the other essentials for a small mine, the drift entrance, lamp cabin, weighbridge to measure the amount of coal coming out of the mine, and a small water source for the colliery engine. The design was drawn on paper at full size and, when I was satisfied that it was what I required, it was inked in as a final plan. When designing layouts I always try to avoid having any track or buildings parallel to the front of the baseboard. Gentle curves are used rather than straight track as it looks more attractive and is easier to lay.

On my track plan I had drawn everything that I needed to construct the track – sleepers, rails, check rails, different types of chairs and all rail gaps. I have nearly always constructed my own track, as I find it frees me from the constraints of the geometry of proprietary commercial track. I used Code 180 bullhead rail, slide-on white-metal chairs and wooden strip sleepers. Since then new materials have become available and I would now use plastic chairs and sleepers. A copy of my track plan was glued onto the cork base and the wooden sleepers glued into position. The white-metal chairs were threaded onto the rail and pinned through the sleepers into the baseboard, the whole process taking about a week.

I am no electrician, but by watching people who can wire up layouts I was able to do enough to get mine working. To power the layout I use an old H&M Duette controller with one outlet powering the tracks and the other the conveyor. The building lights are powered on a separate 20-volt system.

Having a full-size plan of the layout enabled most of the buildings to be constructed off site, knowing that they would fit with only minor adjustments. In the larger scales, having only relatively small areas available for buildings and scenery, they must be small so as not to overwhelm the layout. Most of the buildings on the layout have the style of existing buildings but are much smaller. The main shells of most were constructed from 5mm foam board, giving some depth to the walls and window openings. Brickwork is from thin card, hand-scribed and coloured with terracotta acrylic paint. Roof slates are thin strips of card. I use card and foam board as I have a plentiful supply; I only use plasticard for the fine details. The interiors of most of the buildings have been modelled and interior lighting fitted so that the results of my efforts can be seen easily. The bulbs are 28-volt panel bulbs, about 5mm in diameter, powered by a 24-volt supply. The only large scenic item is the culverted stream under the central part of the layout, which draws the eye towards the centre. The ends of the layout are disguised on the right by the colliery screens and on the left by an overbridge and low-relief shops to disguise the entrance to the fiddle yard.

The conveyor is the main feature of the layout, providing most of the movement and

I have separated this photograph from the previous three because it is a brilliant example of a very effective overall scene. You have the car and the scooter on the bridge in the foreground with the man sitting on the seat, then you have the view unfolding before you right through to the buildings at the far end. The telegraph pole wires in the foreground are particularly convincing and not very often modelled. *Steve Flint, courtesy of Railway Modeller*

'Y9' and a small diesel shunter. These more than suffice as the layout only requires one locomotive. The wagons were hand-built from card and the chassis from commercial parts. I now have four different types of NER hopper wagons.

The layout took just over a year to build and was not too expensive in terms of materials. I really enjoy modelling in the larger scales as I can see what I am doing and can finish a layout in much less time as there are not so many items to construct. At my time of life I am not looking for a 20-year project!

a raison d'être for the running of the trains. I have had working conveyors on most of my layouts but none have been entirely successful, spillage being a common problem.

I had no Gauge 1 rolling stock of my own but managed to borrow an LNER 'Y8', an NER

Bank Hall Sidings (S scale) described by Bill Pearce

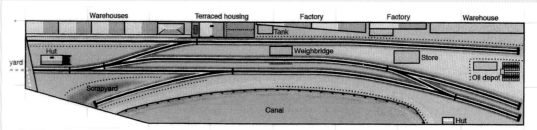

Plan of 'Bank Hall Sidings'

Bank Hall Sidings is another minimum-space layout, this time in S scale. The overall size of the scenic area is 8 feet by 1ft 7in. It was inspired by various sidings and rail-linked industries that were part of the East Lancashire line in the early 1960s. S scale is not commonly used, and is 3/16 inch to 1 foot.

In simple terms, the layout can be described as a freelance industrial layout based in the North West of England.

The locos are the main reason why the actual location is a little vague, but I have used the various sets of etchings and fittings available through the S Scale Society. They are, however,

Above: **A good overall view of 'Bank Hall Sidings'. I think the proprietary back scenes in the distance are very effective, but that may be because I have used them myself on previous layouts!** *Derek Shore*

Below: **I particularly like this photograph of the overgrown tracks on the left with the bridge in the distance and the loco alongside the building on the right. The contrast between the ballasted track on the left and the track on the right is especially effective and realistic.** *Derek Shore*

consistent in their mechanisms and all have split-axle pick-up, high-level gearboxes, flywheels and can motors. The rolling stock is a mixed bag, with items built from S Scale Society etchings or scratch-built using the same source.

The track is hand-built using flat-bottom Code 83 rail to represent the type used in some industrial locations, and is laid to fine-scale dimensions as decided by Ian Pusey. The buildings are also scratch-built, some using computer chads to represent brickwork while other buildings use various Wills and Slaters plastic sheets. Many of the details are actually items intended for other scales but adapted for use on this layout.

Peters Street Station (OO gauge) described by Peter Harvey

The track plan for 'Peters Street Station'

A good 'end-on' view of 'Peters Street Station'. Note the surveyors at work on the left. *Peter Harvey*

'Peters Street Station' represents a small terminus on the east side of Birmingham built on derelict land not far from the West Coast Main Line and on the edge of a new housing estate just outside the green belt. Signalling and points are controlled by the Washwood Heath signal control box.

The layout was designed with transport in mind as I only have a two-door car and did not want to lug a great thing around to and from shows. It is 1 foot wide and 8 feet long when assembled, and weighs 12kg, so I can very easily assemble it on my own. It is controlled using a Lenz LH 100EZ controller or Dynamis. The turnouts and signals are controlled by use of DCC accessory decoders.

The trackwork is Peco Code 100 that has been ballasted and weathered to give a realistic effect. I scratchbuilt as many buildings as I could.

The rolling stock is proprietary but I have fitted lights to some of it, which took a considerable amount of time. I have also repainted some.

The station and the car park. Note the recycling skips on the left, something often seen but rarely modelled. *Peter Harvey*

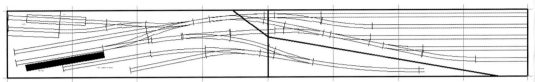

Dudley Road (OO gauge) described by Peter Harvey

The track plan for 'Dudley Road'

'Dudley Road' was photographed at the Sutton Coldfield exhibition in 2009. The pictures show the very effective modelling of the hardstanding and the retaining wall, the detail inside the depot and the locos and tanker wagons outside. *Both Peter Harvey*

Dudley Road represents a small light maintenance depot on the west side of Birmingham built on the remains of an old LMS engine shed/maintenance depot that is now part of an industrial estate not far from the WCML.

The old signal box has gone and the depot is now controlled from the main power box at New Street. Drivers have to ask permission to leave the depot to rejoin the main line after refuelling or maintenance; other movements in the yard are controlled by radio and the New Street power box.

As with 'Peters Street Station', the layout was designed with transport in mind, so the dimensions are identical (8 feet by 1 foot), and it weighs 15kg. One thing I did want was a run-round loop to make shunting operations possible. The layout is controlled by a Lenz LH 100 controller or Dynamis and the turnouts are controlled by use of a probe-and-stud board.

The trackwork is as 'Peters Street Station' and, again, a lot of the buildings are scratch-built. The rolling stock is mainly Class 66 locos, and some departmental wagons and tankers are regularly seen. Many of the locos are fitted with lights.

Polhendra Clay Works (OO gauge) described by Hugh Flynn

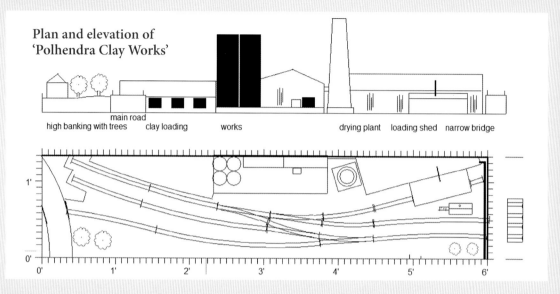

Plan and elevation of 'Polhendra Clay Works'

main road
high banking with trees   clay loading   works   drying plant   loading shed   narrow bridge

Polhendra is a small fictitious clay works located near St Austell. It is situated between two bridges, which is why it is restricted to short freight trains. The layout is set around the year 2000 with train movements carried out using EWS Class 37/60/66 locomotives. There is also a passenger service to the coastal town of Newquay. The buildings are both scratch-built and modified kits based on photos of different buildings and locations.

The trackwork is Peco Code 75 and live-frog points are used in conjunction with Seep point motors. All the track was laid on a cork bed. I like to have the track slightly on a curve as I feel it looks better and more realistic. Once laid, the track was covered with Woodland Scenics extra-fine ballast; when I was happy with it, I used an old washing-up liquid bottle filled with the mixture of 50/50 PVA wood glue and water with a touch of washing-up liquid to fix the ballast in position. The ballast was wetted with a water mist and the mixture dropped over it. This is best done on a nice warm day or in a warm room – if the latter,

An overall view of the layout. Photographs are shown in a digital photoframe fixed to the front of the layout at the top left-hand side. These can be of the prototype or the layout. *Hugh Flynn*

Another overall view, looking towards the right-hand end of the layout – the scenic detail is there for all to see. *Hugh Flynn*

make sure a plastic sheet is put on the floor first! One thing I never do is pin down the track on the scenic part of the layout. My preference is to stick it down with wood glue or Evo-stick, as I find the sleeper usually ends up deformed if you use track pins.

Most of the scenic material used on the layout is Woodland Scenics scatter, clump and foliage, etc. Hornby trees and Ratio fencing separate the railway from the clay works. Wills stone sheets were used for scratch-building the bridges and walls, and the Vari-bridge pack for building the bridges.

The layout is DCC-operated by an NCE Powercab, with most of the locomotives fitted with sound.

George Street Stabling Point Mk 1 (OO gauge) described by Richard Scott

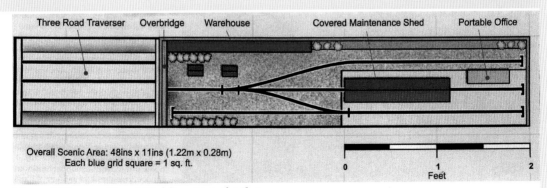

| Three Road Traverser | Overbridge | Warehouse | Covered Maintenance Shed | Portable Office |

Overall Scenic Area: 48ins x 11ins (1.22m x 0.28m)
Each blue grid square = 1 sq. ft.

0   1   2
         Feet

Plan of 'George Street Stabling Point' Mk 1

This layout came into being because, as Exhibition Manager of the Normanton & Pontefract RMS, I noticed the need for a few more modern-image layouts in the show; this was the first layout I built. It is OO gauge and measures 48 inches by 11 inches, plus a 19-inch-long fiddle yard. The baseboard is made from 2 by 1 inch timber with a 6mm

MDF top and a 6mm plywood backscene. The control panel is an integral part of the layout and a KPC controller is used. Points are controlled by Richard's version of the 'wire-in-tube' method.

Structures on the layout come from various sources including Wills, Cooper Craft and Knightwing, and there is some scratch-building using Slaters Plastikard. Locomotives are a mixture of Bachmann, Hornby and Heljan.

If anyone thinks they have no room for an interesting layout, surely this one shows that a good 'cameo' scene can be created on, say, a bookshelf or in the corner of a room, which can also be easily transported to exhibitions. (Having built a number of layouts using an ironing board as the support, I [Nigel Adams] think 'George Street Stabling Point Mk 1' would be ideally suited.)

For those wondering why the layout is called 'Mark 1', the answer is simple. Mark Murray was so impressed when he operated it at exhibitions that he built 'Mark 2', which is described next.

A view looking across the stabling point. I think this is very effective in the way it incorporates different levels from ground level at the front of the fence to the backscene. The foreground detail is good too, and I especially like the inclusion of the fork-lift truck. *Richard Scott*

Another overall view, showing how effective it is when the layout is 'framed', drawing in the viewer's eye. The fascia is also a good way of showing the name of the layout, and is somewhere to display the 'exhibition plaques'. Perhaps this is not surprising, as Richard Scott is the Exhibition Manager for the Normanton & Pontefract RMS! *Richard Scott*

George Street Stabling Point Mk 2 (OO gauge) described by Mark Murray

The idea for this layout came from Richard Scott's 'Mark 1' layout, which I enjoyed operating at exhibitions. However, it was not long enough to enable me to run my Class 66 locomotives, so I built a larger version of it. 'Mark 1' is 48 inches long whereas my layout is 60 inches long and 3 inches wider at 14 inches. The fiddle yard has four roads compared with three on 'Mark 1', and is about twice as long at 36 inches. Like 'Mark 1', it is OO gauge.

All track is Code 100 and the points are electrically controlled using Seep motors. The layout is controlled from the front by the Lenz DCC system. The buildings are kits and modular kits from Pikestuff and Cornerstone.

Both the 'George Street Stabling Point' layouts are good examples of small layouts where the builder has modelled a particular area of the prototype. They look very realistic and could easily be incorporated into a larger layout if the space became available, while still being able to be taken to exhibitions if invited.

A good overall view of the layout at an exhibition. This time the name of the layout takes up the whole of the fascia. You will also notice that, like Hugh Flynn's 'Polhendra Clay Works', the layout is operated from the front. *Richard Scott*

An 'aerial view' looking down on the layout. If you ignore the controller and the crowd barrier you could be looking at the real thing. *Richard Scott*

The following eight layouts were built by Colin French, a prolific builder of small layouts over many years, who also describes them.

Ledsam Street Yard (O gauge) described by Colin French

'Ledsam Street Yard' is a purely fictional O-gauge fine-scale micro shunting layout based on an industrial setting somewhere in the United Kingdom. The layout represents a small area of a much larger industrial complex in the early 1930s period.

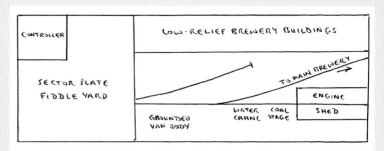

Plan of 'Ledsam Street Yard'

The design was inspired by an article for a small OO-gauge layout entitled 'Balls Yard', which appeared in the August 1992 issue of *Scale Model Trains* but was adapted for my own use and in O gauge. I think the planning of the layout took almost as long as its construction. Sketches were made and pieces of paper cut out to represent wagons and locos, then moved about on the layout to make sure it would work when built and be operationally interesting.

The overall size of the layout is 45 inches by 16 inches. The baseboard is of conventional design with the fiddle yard end having internal framing that allows the layout to be stored on its end when not in use. As three-link couplings are used throughout, a simple 'bolt-on' lighting pelmet is used to ensure that the operator can see to couple and uncouple the rolling stock.

Because there was a need to use sharp curves it was decided to build the track in situ. Peco Code 100 flat-bottom rail soldered to copper-clad sleepers was used, and checkrails are soldered in so that the trackwork can be buried tramway-style and the soldered joints disguised. The point is of 3-foot radius, as are most of the other curves on the layout.

The fiddle yard is a sector plate consisting of a length of soldered track with a single screw fixing at the far end to act as a pivot. Check

A view showing the effective use of kit parts as low-relief buildings. Heljan used to make this engine shed kit and a factory kit, which were very similar. Unfortunately, they have stopped making them and the engine shed kit now produced is much larger. If ever you see any of the old kits for sale, known as Top Link kits, snap them up! *Colin French*

rails are again soldered in, which makes this length of track very rigid. The sector plate is just long enough to hold the largest loco plus one wagon. Other screws are placed at either side of the maximum 'swing' of the sector plate to ensure that it lines up with the appropriate track.

At the front of the layout is a small loco shed with the usual basic facilities. The middle siding gives access to a brewery, while the back siding is used for servicing the brewery engineer, quality control and cooperage departments.

The 0-4-0 loco is about to leave the yard. Note the low-relief wall and bridge and the grounded van body. *Colin French*

The buildings at the back of the layout are modelled in half relief from a Top Link kit (sadly no longer available). The loco shed is from a Heljan kit, the grounded van body is from Slaters and the coal stage is an Invertrain kit. The working yard lights are Viessmann HO models, but they look right in this setting. Other details are mainly Duncan castings.

Wagons are mainly Parkside kits with a couple of Websters (now Peco) GWR kits included.

I have a small collection of 0-4-0 and short-wheelbase 0-6-0 tank engines, both industrial and main-line, which are used. For exhibitions the main locos are an LSWR 'B4' (Vulcan kit) in Southampton Docks 1935 brown livery and an Andrew Barclay 0-4-0T (Tower Models).

For home operations, six wagons are used on the layout plus a loco coal wagon as 'nuisance value'. Each of the wagons has a card with its description written on it and the cards are numbered 1 to 6. A dice is thrown to select three wagons – two for the middle siding and one for the back siding – the loco coal wagon having to be moved to suit. There is a penalty whenever the loco coal wagon is away from the loco coal stage, apart from the beginning and end of the shunting session, when room has to be found in the back siding for this wagon to allow access for the locomotive to and from the locomotive shed. Any new wagon coming on to the layout has to be positioned before outgoing wagons are removed. This can provide a lengthy shunting session and allows continual operational interest for such a small layout.

At exhibitions only four wagons are used plus the loco coal wagon, and these are shunted in rotation, two wagons for the middle siding and one for the back siding, with the loco coal wagon having to be moved to suit. Again, there is an imaginary penalty whenever the loco coal wagon is away from the coaling stage, but something is always 'on the move' for the paying public to see, which, I feel, is important.

Why the name 'Ledsam Street'? This is the street where I was born in a well-known railway town and the layout had to be called something.

Who hasn't got room for a model railway!

2 into 1 (O gauge) described by Colin French

This layout is built to a scale of 7mm to 1 foot and shows what can be achieved in this scale in a very small space. The whole board measures 48 inches by 15 inches and is mounted on a television turntable.

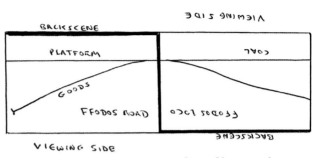

Plan of '2 into 1'

The baseboard is divided into two parts with a different layout on each side of the divider, each acting as a fiddle yard for the other. The idea came from an article in the February 1996 issue of *Railway Modeller*. Only two turnouts, one curved section and three straight sections of track are used, which are all Rivarossi purchased second-hand several years ago.

One end of the layout is **Ffodos Loco**, which represents a small locomotive shed with the usual facilities somewhere in the United Kingdom at an industrial concern. The factory's own locos are seen with an occasional visit from a main-line shunting locomotive. Locomotives arrive for servicing then depart to continue with their work.

The other end is **Ffodos Road**, a Light Railway terminus as part of the Colonel Stephens empire. Unfortunately the line has fallen on hard times and passenger services were withdrawn some time ago. However, the local farmer's cooperative warehouse adjacent to the small goods yard still generates much freight traffic, so the line has been truncated here to serve this facility and the local community for goods traffic. The station building is used as an office by the local freight clerk-cum-shunter and the grounded van body serves as a lock-up goods store. Nature has already taken over the buffer stops and is slowly encroaching on the yard and platform as well!

Below left: **A view showing the front of the larger Heljan engine shed kit used as a very effective backscene on 'Ffodos Loco'. It shows that you do not have to build the shed for the locos to actually enter.** *Colin French*

The very detailed yard and station at 'Ffodos Road'. *Colin French*

Dock Green Loco (O gauge) described by Colin French

This layout is a fictional O-gauge, 7mm to 1 foot minimum-space layout measuring 1 metre by 0.5 metre, and based on a locomotive servicing facility where a loco shed used to exist but has now been closed.

The backscene represents dockland warehouses and the endscene is the original loco shed. All other services at the loco depot survive, thus providing adequate facilities for visiting freight tank locos and, occasionally, the Dock Company's own locos. At the other end of the layout is the Dock Lane overbridge, which provides the scenic break.

The layout consists of three parallel tracks, two of which are the loco depot and the third a hidden siding. To save space there are no turnouts on the layout. A short traverser is used in the fiddle yard to enable locos to change tracks.

The period depicted is the 1920s and the location is the dockland area of East London. Locomotives seen are those that regularly worked goods trains into the docks from the newly formed LMS and LNER, mostly via the

North London Railway during this period, when some were still wearing their pre-Grouping livery. The Dock Company's own locos are also seen occasionally.

This is the view looking towards the shed. Again, Heljan large engine shed kit parts have been used on the right. The coaling stage and the pit are most effective. *Colin French*

Ffodos Treacle Works (O gauge) described by Colin French

Plan of 'Ffodos Treacle Works'

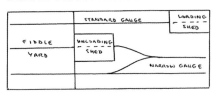

Probably the best-kept secret of Mid Suffolk was the Ffodos Treacle Mine. A rich seam of black treacle ore was first discovered here on 1 April 1907. The Treacle Works was built a short distance from the mine where the land was a bit more stable, and was connected to the mine by a narrow-gauge horse-worked tramway. Treacle was mined here right up until the late 1950s, when foreign imports

outpriced the locally mined treacle. Black treacle ore looks very similar to coal, and if the two minerals are mistakenly confused disastrous consequences can occur!

There was a brief interruption to mining activities during the middle of the Second World War when the USAAF took over the mine as an ammunition store for local airfields. During this time the United States Army Transportation Corps rebuilt the tramway and introduced its own diesel-powered locomotives to move the equipment and stores.

At the end of hostilities mining recommenced and the company took over the running of the tramway, acquiring two of the small refurbished American diesels to provide the motive power. As there was a steep rope-worked incline from the mine to the tramway, only two 'tubs' or wagons are hauled up at any one time, hence the short trains. The works were connected to the main line in Needham Market goods yard by a standard-gauge connection. Main-line locomotives work the standard-gauge connection, which is very lightly laid.

The layout measures 48 inches by 18 inches in 7mm scale and shows the narrow-gauge tramway connection to the mine, where loaded 'tubs' are brought to the works, shunted into the unloading shed and emptied; the empty 'tubs' are taken back to the mine. The working can be quite intense, with both the diesels working at peak times. At the back of the layout is the rest of the works where the black treacle ore is processed into edible treacle and finally conveyed out in barrels or drums in covered or sheeted wagons on the standard-gauge track. The period depicted

is around the end of the Second World War, when the mine and works were brought back into use.

An overall view showing the standard-gauge and narrow-gauge tracks and rolling stock. *Colin French*

Foxbile Brewery (O gauge) described by Colin French

'Foxbile Brewery' (a Spoonerism of 'box file') is a minimum-space shunting layout in O gauge (7mm to 1 foot), constructed in two box files plus a little extra at the back for a hidden siding. There are no points, similar to one of my other layouts, which saves space.

It is envisaged that this small country brewery has enough work for the sidings to be continually shunted, and both the LMS and LNER have interests there. Only

Colin French presides over the operation of 'Foxbile Brewery'. Who says you can't model in 7mm scale in a small space? *Colin French collection*

A real close-up! The shunter talks to the driver of the Sentinel loco. The use of short locos is one of the secrets of building small layouts.
Colin French

four wagons are used and the operation requires that each wagon is moved one space anti-clockwise each time a sequence is carried out. The locomotive used is either an LMS or LNER small shunter, normally a Sentinel, but others can be seen from time to time. The period depicted is the 1930s.

The Wagon Works (O gauge) described by Colin French

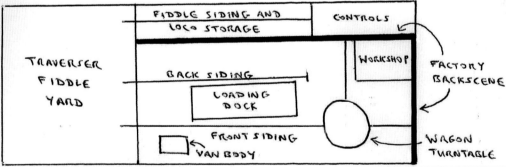

Plan of 'The Wagon Works'

This layout is a fictional O-gauge minimum-space shunting layout based on a railway workshop setting somewhere in the United Kingdom, but influenced by what the builder remembers of Wolverton Works in the town where he was born. The layout measures 49 inches by 19 inches.

The backscene represents workshops, which are served by a working wagon turntable and shunted by rope or chain and capstan to create a bit more interest. To save space, there are no turnouts on the layout.

Four wagons are used at exhibitions, and locomotives depend on the location and period chosen. There are various tank engines from the appropriate companies and those associated with railway workshops during the chosen period, which is the mid-1930s.

A nice shot of a small 0-4-0 in the yard in front of the crane and wheel-sets in the foreground. Again, Heljan parts are used in the background. *Colin French*

The wagon turntable can be seen in the left foreground. Note the stack of timber with the man and the cat, and the tin roof on the building behind them. *Colin French*

The next four layouts were built and are described by Mike Bragg.

Lenches Bridge (O gauge) described by Mike Bragg

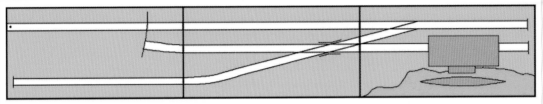

Plan of 'Lenches Bridge'

Space or lack of it in our modest home meant that although I was going to model in O gauge it would have to be a small layout and portable. I had joined the Gauge O Guild and read its booklet on small layouts, but a chance visit to Carl Arendt's wonderful

Note the derelict building on the left of the photograph. Again, derelict buildings are often seen but not often modelled and, when they are and done well as they are here, they certainly add to the realism we are trying to achieve. *Mike Bragg*

website led me to 'Box Street', a layout plan by Jack Trollope. I flipped the design over and, hey presto, 'Lenches Bridge'. I opted for an overall size of 9 feet by 1ft 9in on three baseboards, two of 3ft 6in and one of 2 feet. The layout consists of one left-hand point and a double-slip. One board has the point, the centre board the slip, and the third the sector plate – like me, it's simple!

There were a number of things that I wanted to incorporate in the model. One was a silted-up canal basin with a half-submerged 'Joey', as seen during my childhood in Stourbridge

Town goods yard and around Bromley Basin. Others were an out-of-use transhipment shed, a derelict pump house, a brick works and a Baggeridge Coal Wharf. These features were all to be found on the Kingswinford Railway, or the 'Old Worse and Worse' (Oxford, Worcester & Wolverhampton Railway) and the lines around Shut End, Lenches Bridge and Ashwood Basin. I decided to set the layout in the 1950s just after nationalisation, as I remember the locations as somewhat tired and run down, a bit like me now.

An overall view of 'Lenches Bridge' looking towards the fiddle yard. I particularly like the roof on the building with the hole in it and the sunken barge in the foreground.
Mike Bragg

Looking in the opposite direction, note how the fiddle yard is hidden by the low-relief building in front of it. Note also the high level at the back of the layout with the fence on the embankment. This adds depth to the narrow board.
Mike Bragg

Ashwood Basin (O gauge) described by Mike Bragg

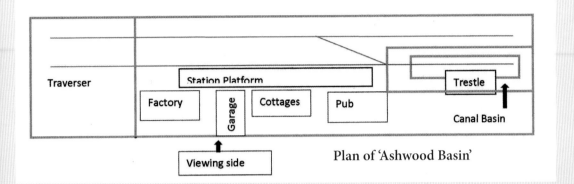

Plan of 'Ashwood Basin'

Ashwood Basin was on the Staffordshire & Worcestershire Canal and was the western terminus of the Earl of Dudley's

Note the fence with planks missing - so often seen but not often modelled. This really adds to the realism we are seeking. *Mike Bragg*

railway system, which opened in 1829. Today, virtually all signs of the railway tracks have disappeared and it is now a marina for pleasure craft. From Ashwood Basin the line ran to Shut End, and the collieries at Corbyns Hall near Lenches Bridge. The railway's main purpose was to convey coal to the canal, and

A good view of the simple platform and waiting shelter at Ashwood Basin. *Mike Bragg*

Looking from the other side of the platform, we see the canal basin at the end of the baseboard, which gives the layout its name. *Mike Bragg*

this continued until the NCB stopped sending Baggeridge coal to Stourport Power Station via the canal in October 1953.

In building the baseboards I took into account the lie of the land and decided on a sloping site down to canal. I also decided that the railway would be very much in the landscape, not dominating it. Baseboard construction followed the methods used on

Lenches Bridge: good-quality planed softwood framing cut using a cross-cut saw to ensure the ends were square, finished with a ply top, and all glued and screwed together. The layout is 9 feet by 21 inches and is set over the two boards with the scenic section covering all of one and about a third of the other, the rest of the second board being a traverser running on ball-bearing slides.

Pattingham (O gauge) described by Mike Bragg

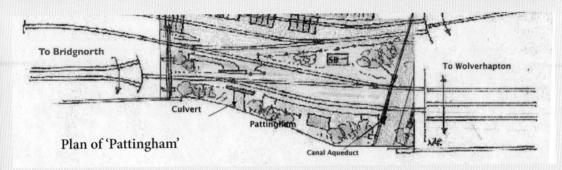

To Bridgnorth

SB

To Wolverhapton

Culvert

Pattingham

Plan of 'Pattingham'

Canal Aqueduct

I take no credit for the track plan as this is the work of Neil Ripley ('Rippers') and the 1059 group from Hull MRC. They created 'St Minions' in EM gauge in about 2ft 6in plus

A short train enters the yard at Pattingham. Note the aqueduct, partly visible, in the top right-hand corner, a feature not very often modelled. *Mike Bragg*

fiddle yards, while I went for 4ft 6in in 7mm, again plus fiddle yards. The scenic board (B) is 4ft 6in long and 2 feet wide where it joins Fiddle Yard A, and 2ft 6in wide where it joins Fiddle Yard C. Fiddle Yard A measures 3ft 6in by 2 feet and Fiddle Yard C 3ft 6in by 2ft 6in.

The basic scenery consists of the sandstone outcrops at each end of the main board made from plywood and card formers with a plaster

An 0-6-0 pannier tank and two vans stand at the other end of the layout. *Mike Bragg*

bandage shell. The sandstone is made from Hydrocal plaster and home-made moulds, stained with a mixture of Brake Dust and Burnt Sienna. Ground cover is a mixture of Woodland Scenics and flock from a home-made electrostatic spreader (a converted fly swat). The hardstanding is thin ply and filler painted with Tamiya Deck Tan and weathered with a thin wash of greys and browns.

There is nothing special about the buildings and associated structures, which have ply inner shells with plasticard skins.

The station building is based on a William Eassie design, and although the originals were of timber construction I have opted for brick. The aqueduct is a simple version of the Edstone aqueduct on the Stratford-on-Avon Canal, while the pipe bridge is based on the one at Gornal, which carried the South Staffs main water line. To get the red-brown brick effect, the structures were first sprayed with a yellow filler primer then, when dry, Humbrol Brick Red was applied and almost rubbed off.

Spinners End (O gauge) described by Mike Bragg

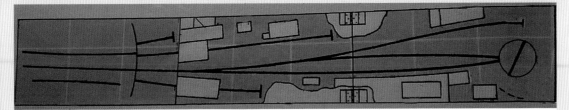

Plan of 'Spinners End'

With this layout I went back to my Earl of Dudley theme and started a new project. The layout plan is a mirror-image of 'Alfriston' from Volume 1 of the *Small Layout Book* from the Gauge O Guild.

'Grandad?'

'Yes, sweetheart.'

'What's that turning thing at the end of the station?'

'It's a turntable. It allows engines to change from one track to another.'

'Oh, I thought it was so that they could spin round.' And with that she went back into the house.

That simple question now had me thinking – why not call the layout 'Spinners End' rather than my original name 'Saltwells'? Spinners End happened to be a goods depot at the end of the Corn Greaves branch from Cradley Heath, not that far from Saltwells, and it also happens to be the name of the Muggle street where Severus Snape lives in the Harry Potter books, so how could I not use it?

The turntable at the end of the baseboard is a great space-saver because a point and a headshunt are avoided. It is also an added attraction at exhibitions. *Mike Bragg*

At the other end of 'Spinners End' are the loco shed and the auto-coach in its carriage shed. *Mike Bragg*

Like its predecessors, 'Mount Pleasant', 'Lenches Bridge', 'Ashwood Basin' and 'Pattingham', 'Spinners End' is set in the Black Country and is part of what was once the Earl of Dudley's rail system. Of course, true to form I have massaged, bent and stretched the facts to suit my needs, so no surprise there, then…

The layout has been built to a 9 feet by 18 inches footprint on three baseboards. The 6-foot scenic section folds in half to form a box, and the fiddle yard is bolted on to this section. The front panel folds down so that the hinge assembly does not stand proud of the layout surface, so no overbridge or building is needed to conceal it.

These next three layouts were built and are described by Nick Palette.

Tremore (OO gauge) described by Nick Palette

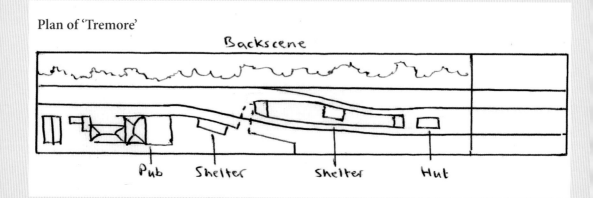

Plan of 'Tremore'

Backscene

Pub   Shelter   Shelter   Hut

'Tremore' came about from a desire to build a small layout that fulfilled two objectives, that it could be easily carried, and that it would have the appearance of a three-dimensional picture. Inspiration came from the china clay branches around St Blazey and the Newquay branch; however, it was decided to situate the layout on the former LSWR lines near Bodmin.

The layout measures 66 by 10 inches and consists of a small station platform with

An overall view of Tremore, showing how the layout is 'framed'; this is good for exhibitions as it focuses the viewers' attention on the model rather than the surrounding area. *Nick Palette*

An EWS freight enters the station. *Nick Palette*

sidings behind. The track layout was arrived at after much agonising as to how to include both the passenger and freight lines. Like the proverbial light bulb suddenly going on, I realised that they did not necessarily have to be connected as I had first envisaged.

The pictorial aspect was achieved by not including the traditional backscene, which gives an unnatural 'straight line' effect to the sky. Instead, at the suggestion of Chris Gilbert,

I cut a tree profile on the backscene and this provided a much more natural sightline.

Operations are normally set in the 21st century with trains from EWS and Wessex Trains. However, it is an ambition to vary the era with the possibility of stepping back in time to, say, the 1970s (blue diesels) or the 1960s (SR steam). The layout is DCC-operated via a Lenz 100 system, although the one point is hand-operated.

North Plains (HO gauge) described by Nick Palette

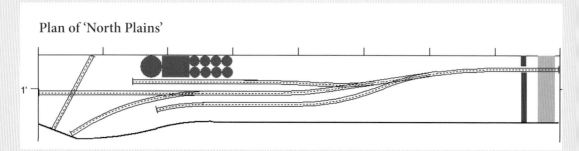

Plan of 'North Plains'

'North Plains' is an attempt to model a US-based layout but to break away from the typical switching (shunting) layout that we so often see. As part of this thinking, I wanted to model the wide open spaces with very little track, and not fall into the trap of cramming as much as possible into the space with spurs (sidings) everywhere, each serving an industry, with the result that a layout looks like a page from the Walthers catalogue!

The layout measures 12 feet in length by 18 inches wide at its widest point. The track plan is an 'inglenook' with an additional siding that forms part of the simulated interchange. There is also a 4-foot-long section that provides an open staging (fiddle) yard. This is a concept I had not

tried before, always previously hiding the staging area, but it works very well.

To provide the feeling of openness, there is no backscene. Also, to get away from the more popular areas (Florida, the South West, West Coast, etc) and the more popular

Above and opposite bottom: These two views of 'North Plains' from opposite ends show how effective it is in portraying the larger American locos and rolling stock in a small space not usually associated with American layouts. *Nick Palette*

railroads, I decided to look at the small Arkansas & Missouri, which, as the name implies, runs in those states. I was able, via the internet, to obtain sufficient (some might say too much!) motive power already painted for the A&M. Rolling stock was not an issue as the prototype road interchanges at each end are with the 'big boys' (UP and BNSF), so most of the traffic is received in cars from those roads and their predecessors.

Lochnagar (OO gauge) described by Nick Palette

Plan of 'Lochnagar'

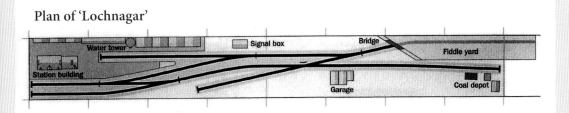

I had for a long time wanted to model something Scottish. This was fuelled by personal visits and magazine articles, particularly those over the years from Ian Futers. When Heljan introduced its Class 26 and 27 locomotives, there was no excuse left not to do it.

The layout was initially designed to be complete (including fiddle yard) on two 4 by 1 foot sections. This meant that the fiddle yard was a single siding behind the visible coal siding, with stock being changed by hand. After the first exhibition it became all too apparent that this was not at all satisfactory.

A freight train enters and a passenger train leaves Lochnagar. *Both Nick Palette*

A third section, 3 feet long, was therefore built to accommodate a three-track fiddle yard. As the longest train was a Class 26 and two Mk 1 coaches, this just fitted into the longest siding, leaving the other two shorter sidings for the freight and a DMU.

The layout followed traditional construction using Peco Code 100 track and large-radius points. A large amount of realism was achieved with careful ballasting and colouring. On many occasions I have been asked at exhibitions about the track, and most people are amazed that it is standard Peco Streamline.

Warmley (OO gauge) described by Neil Burgess

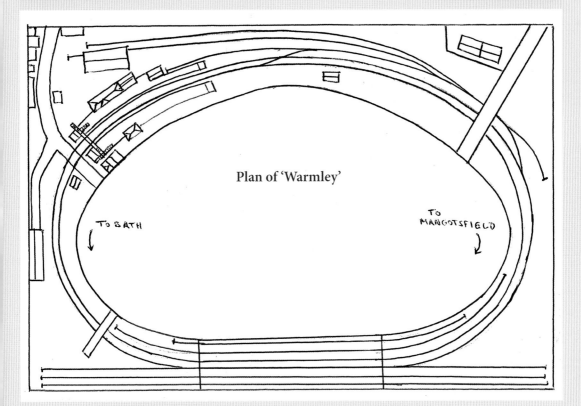

Plan of 'Warmley'

TO BATH

TO MANGOTSFIELD

Railways are creatures of habit: anyone who has spent much time observing a section of almost any line will recognise this. Trains run at set times, comprising generally similar types of vehicles and locomotives; the equipment works in predictable ways, the staff likewise. Anyone who wants to play a part in operating a railway needs to become attuned to its rhythms and patterns, its customs and practices. People say they can set their watches by the passage of trains and this, in general, is so. From time to time the unpredicted or unusual event disturbs the pattern, but it is all the more noticeable because of the change from the commonplace.

Model railways, if they are to be believable, need to embody these habitual features of the real thing. It is as important to replicate the measured routine by which the railway went about its business as it is to have correct track layouts and signalling or the right types of locomotives and rolling stock – not least because all of these contribute to the character of the model and its ability to convey the feel of the prototype.

When I was a child, Warmley, on the

Above: A very realistic picture of a train coming under the bridge towards Warmley station. The 'dirtying' of the arches to represent the smoke staining from passing trains is well done. *Neil Burgess*

Below: A passenger train rounds the curve, with vans and wagons in the yard to the left. The signal is very effective and really adds to the realism, as does the tall building in the background. *Neil Burgess*

Midland Railway's Bath extension of 1869, was our nearest station. Shopping trips to Bath often began with a bus ride from home and a short wait on the platform for the train, generally of three coaches pulled by a BR Class 3 tank engine, usually Nos 82001, 82004 or 82041, to draw in and take us to the Midland station, then called Green Park. When I was older I would sometimes go down to the station on summer evenings and watch the last passenger trains of the day pass through, together with the trip goods from Bath to Westerleigh marshalling yard, about 7 miles further north, hauled by one of the last Somerset & Dorset 7F 2-8-0s, most usually No 53807. Later still I got to know the signalmen and was able – entirely unofficially – to try my hand at working the box; something that stood me in good stead when, much more recently, I became a traffic volunteer on the Talyllyn Railway. Even now, more than 40 years later, I can recall the sights of those times, and the regular passage of the trains, which came to an abrupt and final end in March 1966 when the line closed, together with the Somerset & Dorset route from Bath to Bournemouth, with which it connected.

Of the layout structure there is little to be said. It is OO gauge finescale, and measures 12 by 8 feet; it was not intended to be exhibited. The boards are 6mm ply, the frames being made on the 'sandwich beam' principle pioneered by Barry Norman, which allows the inner edge of the structure to be curved in a somewhat squat ellipse, as shown on the plan. Track is SMP bullhead with points from similar rail and copper-clad Paxolin sleepers. Signals are from Model Signal Engineering parts and almost all the structures are scratch-built, mostly in either card or plastic sheet. At least one of the bridges I measured up in 1970, and was thus finally able to use those long-stored details – you never know when these things will come in handy! Shoehorning a secondary main line into a room 8 feet by 12 feet took a bit of careful planning, but I was greatly encouraged by a similar project by the late David Jenkinson, who recreated Dent, alias 'Garsdale Road', on the Settle-Carlisle line – the other end of the Midland, in fact – in a space only slightly larger.

The trains themselves were modelled from details built up by studying lots of photographs. Unlike the Somerset & Dorset line, the Midland's Bath extension received very little attention from most photographers, but those who did were most helpful and a picture was built up of the appearance and pattern of the trains and the locomotives that pulled them. The layout is worked to a 24-hour sequence taken directly from the 1954 working timetable and this gives not only the 'feel' of the prototype but also avoids operation becoming simply a random selection of trains that run because it's a while since the last one. Most of the traffic over the line was either stopping passenger trains running between Bristol and Bath, with about half continuing to Bournemouth over the S&D line, or else trip goods workings between Westerleigh yard and Bath. In addition there were four longer-distance goods trains, three to Washwood Heath yard and the other to Lawley Street goods depot in Birmingham.

The most prestigious trains of the day were the up and down workings of the 'Pines Express', which ran daily between Manchester London Road and Bournemouth. In connection with the 'Pines' were two parcels workings. The 12.40am Leicester London Road-Bath was worked from Birmingham by the engine that returned from Bath at noon with the up 'Pines', while the engine that worked the down 'Pines' into Bath around 2.40pm returned north with the 8.25pm Templecombe-Derby perishables. There is something very satisfying about recreating these long-gone workings, all the more so when, as recently, I was provided with details of the Derby perishables' compositions by fellow enthusiast Brian Macdermott.

There is plenty of scope for special workings. Most young men during the 1950s did two years of National Service and there were plenty of occasions when large groups of them needed to be transported around the country. Special goods workings, including fertiliser trains from the chemical works around Avonmouth to the country districts of

Somerset & Dorset, were a feature of the time. Unusual engines might turn up on the line from time to time, including BR 'Britannias', rebuilt 'Royal Scots', LNWR 'Super D' 0-8-0s and 'Austerity' 2-8-0s, together with several Western Region types, but these need to be seen occasionally if the sense of regularity is to be preserved. The Somerset & Dorset line saw many extra passenger trains between the Midlands and the South Coast, particularly on summer Saturdays, and these too can be reproduced.

Warmley is set in 1954 – around the end of March or beginning of April. If this sounds a bit pedantic to some, I find it helps focus the model and its composition. By that time all the

British Railways standard steam classes had appeared and were to remain in production until 1960, but it is before the launch of the Modernisation Plan in the following year. There were still a lot of pre-Grouping locomotives and rolling stock around in 1954, but many were set to vanish in the following years. Much though I like travelling on modern trains, I cannot say I care for diesels as modelling subjects, so not having Pilot Scheme types to model is no hardship.

All in all, I am pleased with 'Warmley' and feel that it captures something of the sense of a place I knew long ago, in what now seems a very different world indeed.

Merlinwood (O gauge) described by John Ross

Plan of 'Merlinwood'

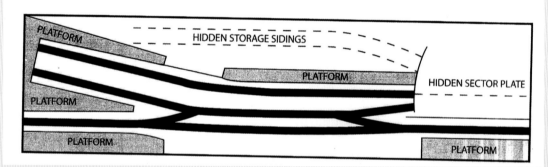

Merlinwood was built by Mike Cole, who sadly died in 2011. I was offered the layout and the opportunity to buy the rolling stock, which was built and painted specifically for 'Merlinwood'.

The layout, in O gauge, represents part of a large Ministry of Defence establishment, and the idea came from observing the workings of the Bicester Military Railway in Oxfordshire in the late 1980s and early 1990s. The large Ordinance Depot at Bicester used a fleet of small diesel locos specially purchased from Thomas Hill Ltd to shunt a variety of mainly vintage short-wheelbase vans and wagons between the numerous warehouses on the site.

'Merlinwood' is located somewhere in

Wessex and is responsible for the receipt, storage and distribution of the mundane but essential supplies necessary for the day-to-day operation and wellbeing of the armed forces. This means that the depot has a very low security rating and, although organised and managed by the MOD, employs a mainly civilian workforce.

The layout measures 8 feet by 2 feet and is set during the 1950s or 1960s. The locomotive fleet – unlike that at Bicester – is a mixture of BR and second-hand diesels, with a variety of visiting steam and diesel locomotives. The visiting locos belong to a local preservation society, and there are specials that work from the main line at weekends.

An overall view of Merlinwood taken at a show at York. *John Ross*

Since I acquired the layout I have carried out additional work on it as it was not quite finished when Mike Cole died. Various small details have been added, such as 'clutter' and maintenance crews. It is exhibited under the auspices of the Solihull Model Railway Circle, details of which can be found on the Circle's website.

Teesside Steel (O gauge) described by Jeff Wetherall

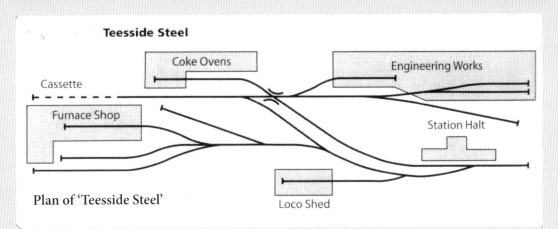

Plan of 'Teesside Steel'

The layout is 7mm scale, O gauge, and is 19 feet long by 2 feet wide. It is prototype/freelance, in that all the buildings and processes are models of the original structures, but the actual arrangement of the various items is freelance in order to fit everything on the layout so that the operation is both interesting and not too cluttered. The model is set in the 1950s to early 1960s to show the steel industry as it was before the widespread rationalisation and demolition during the 1960s and 1970s resulted in fewer but larger and more efficient steel-producing plants that became the core of the British Steel Corporation. The model has been exhibited around the UK, chiefly in Scotland, but also in the North of England and the Midlands.

'Teesside Steel' came into being partly as a change from the usual terminus/through station, and partly to recreate the scenes

Right: Just look at the portrayal of the rust on the buildings in the background. It is so realistic! *Jeff Wetherall*

Below and far right: Models such as 'Teesside Steel' are few and far between, and the specialist rolling stock needed for such layouts is well portrayed in these photographs, together with the various unique structures of the site in the background. *Both Jeff Wetherall*

of industry in the area in which I grew up. Researching the steel industry of the 1950s, I found that many of the old blast furnaces were only producing 40 to 50 tons of iron a day. Consequently, the furnaces were small and could be modelled full size, even in 7mm scale. Many photographs of the plant and buildings were acquired and suitable structures were chosen for final modelling. It was decided at an early stage to model two aspects of the steel industry: the iron and steel making processes, and the heavy engineering plants involved in steel construction, such as bridge-building and other large-scale structures. This meant that a fair number of specialist rail wagons would be required, either from kits or scratch-built.

The track plan is designed to give two operators some interesting operation, each having access to a run-round loop and five

sidings providing a variety of wagons and products. All points are electrically operated, together with working semaphore arms and shunt signals. No interlocking is provided, so operation has to be carried out with a certain amount of care and cooperation.

The left-hand end of the layout (viewed from the front) shows the South Durham Steel & Iron Company, comprising an open-hearth furnace shop with part of a rolling mill, a coke oven complex complete with a by-products loading gantry, as well as a blast furnace and its attendant hot blast stoves and dust extraction plant. A carefully chosen photograph of a complete furnace line is used on the backscene to enhance the overall effect. This, and a photograph of Roseberry Topping, a well-known landmark on the North Yorkshire Moors often seen from the industrial heartland of Teesside on a good day, are the only 'scenic' areas of the backscene. The rest is purely sky, and one end heralds the approach of a gathering storm!

The large building housing the open-hearth furnaces was, of necessity, built from 6mm plywood for strength, and covered with embossed corrugated plastic sheeting suitably painted and 'rusted'. To add a little interest, a working roller shutter door has been constructed to allow hot-metal wagons to enter and leave. Each time the door opens, red warning lights flash to alert the unwary. The coke oven building was shortened to fit the allocated space and was also constructed with plywood covered with embossed sheeting, this time of brick. In common with the prototype, this was suitably 'dirtied'; the only thing missing is the distinctive, unpleasant odour!

The final unit in this section is the furnace line. This was built from a variety of cardboard tubes, including whisky bottle containers (previously emptied of their contents!), aluminium foil rolls and the ubiquitous toilet roll. All were covered with some steel grey paper provided by a friend and, like everything else, suitably 'dirtied' and 'rusted' using a mixture of dry-brushing, weathering powders and a little light spray painting. The remainder of the plant was put together using plastic and copper tubes, an assortment of 'steel' sections and other suitable odds and ends from the scrap box.

The very large building taking up most of the right-hand end of the layout is the Cleveland Bridge & Engineering Company, which provides the heavy engineering side of the steel industry. This is also constructed from the same materials as the other buildings, namely plywood and embossed corrugated sheeting – rather a lot of it in fact! Inside this building can be seen several welders and other workers together with a small forge and a bridge section under construction. The interior is lit, albeit a little dim, as are some of the other structures on the layout such as the signal cabin and loco shed, both of which are fully fitted with all the necessary interior fittings.

Outside this building are two different but nevertheless necessary areas that complete the scene. The first is the steel stockyard, which provides the various plates and sections for the welders to complete their fabrications within the shed. The yard crane is one of the few kits on the layout and depicts a type commonly found in this area during the 1950s. Adjoining the stockyard is the station halt, provided by a grateful management to ensure that the workforce have no difficulty in travelling to and from their place of work in the most efficient manner. Unfortunately, the only available transport at present is a rather dilapidated pair of ex-North Eastern Railway four-wheel coaches. The discrimination between the management and workers on the platform is somewhat obvious!

To create further interest a number of scenic dioramas

are provided, such as a somewhat dilapidated tea shack, an excavation with (some) work in progress, and a certain amount of exterior maintenance on the large engineering shed. Most of the figures on the layout are posed to give the impression that not a lot of work is being done; something that visitors generally find amusing! Allied to this is the fact that working practices in this period left a lot to be desired with regard to safety, and this will be evident in several scenarios around the layout. The token Health & Safety Officer can be seen looking rather bewildered and unsure where to start. Other scenes involve a number of the ubiquitous works cats and several groups of seagulls making a general nuisance of themselves.

At an early show with this layout I was mildly berated by an observant lady who had noticed the plethora of itinerant gulls, but a complete lack of associated avian deposits on the roofs and handrails. Recourse was made to the growing collection of photographs, and at the next exhibition the error had been fully rectified and the lady was most appreciative of the result.

The building of the steel works has required the construction of a large number of specialist vehicles for steel-carrying in either its molten form or various types of finished steel. Most of these have been produced from kits, some plastic but most from etched brass with the

What really makes 'Teesside Steel' such a marvellous layout in my opinion is the attention to detail. Here among the large buildings and all the grime and dirt is the simple platform with the passengers – of all classes! – waiting for their train.
Jeff Wetherall

odd one from white metal. These wagons have varied from short-wheelbase pig-iron carriers through the long-wheelbase plate and trestle wagons up to the big bogie bolsters and trestle vehicles. The very specialised vehicles, the slag ladles, were built from American brass kits modified to British standards and fit (buffers, etc), carrying very realistic loads. The hot-metal wagons utilised American chassis with scratch-built tops.

The main item, the metal-carrier, was made from a plastic wine glass with assorted bits of plastic for detailing and 'Anglicising' of the chassis. These wagons also carry a realistic cargo of molten metal for the open-hearth furnaces, which, at exhibitions, does have some visitors putting out their hands to see if it really is hot! Because of the harsh conditions endured by these vehicles it has been necessary to faithfully copy the state of

the wagons in respect to dirt (filth?), rust and general decrepitude. It is not often one gets to really 'go to town' with so much vigour and enthusiasm to turn a pristine model into one that faithfully replicates the abused and worn condition of the real thing without someone complaining that the effect has been overdone.

Overall, the model is as complete and accurate as I have been able to construct using the information and photographic sources to which I have had access. The three years that it took to make were both enjoyable and challenging as this was my first solo foray into 7mm scale modelling after nearly 40 years in the smaller scales. The end result, however, has been worth all the effort, as the layout has been very well received at each exhibition it has attended and has been a pleasure to operate. I just wonder if the next layout will achieve as much.

Waterhulme (OO9 scale/OO gauge) described by Ian Drummond

Plan of 'Waterhulme'

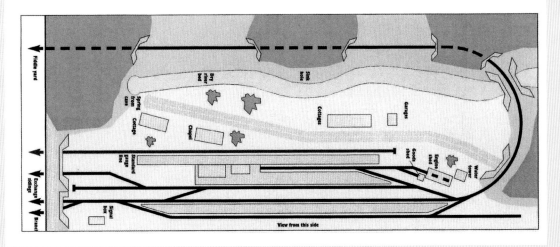

Modelled in OO9 scale/OO gauge, the layout occupies a space of 9ft 9in by 2ft 3in, the scenic section being 6ft 6in wide.

Waterhulme station is on the fictitious Ashbourne & Bakewell Railway, and is based

loosely on Waterhouses station on the former Leek & Manifold Railway in Derbyshire. The main difference is that at the original Waterhouses station the standard gauge was at a higher level, with the narrow gauge below it. It is modelled in the year 1965, when the Ashbourne & Bakewell had been operated by a preservation society for ten years.

After leaving the station, the narrow gauge crosses the dry bed of the River Hulme, the water having disappeared down a 'sink-hole', which is a general characteristic of rivers in limestone country. The line passes through a short tunnel before it emerges on the section, known as 'the high line', based on the Aberglaslyn Pass in Wales. Now the track passes through another short tunnel, before finally disappearing through the hills to Bakewell.

At the time being modelled, the British Railways line is still open, with a service provided by either a single-car or two-car DMU. The station has been 'rationalised', with the run-round loop dismantled, and the station buildings have been boarded up prior to being demolished.

A characteristic of the original Leek & Manifold Railway was its use of transporter wagons to move standard-gauge wagons along the line. The Ashbourne & Bakewell also has one of these in service. Originally the line was built with a colonial feel, and the locomotives operated on the line reflect a variety of origins from both home and overseas. The model is now nearly 20 years old and has been exhibited all over the United Kingdom and in Germany.

An ex-Cyprus Railway 4-4-0 locomotive rounds the curve into Waterhulme past the engine shed and the scaffolding tower where a BBC Television crew are doing a live outside broadcast. The locomotive is a Roxey Mouldings kit on a Graham Farish chassis. The engine shed model is now some 20 years old, which explains its somewhat ramshackle look. *Ian Drummond*

The driver of an ex-Cyprus Railway 2-6-2T checks the signal before entering the final tunnel on the curve into Waterhulme, while a seagull looks on disinterestedly from the cottage chimneys. *Ian Drummond*

Cornwallis Yard (EM gauge)
described by David and Alison Barker

Plan of 'Cornwallis Yard'

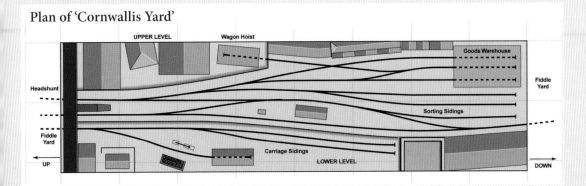

We are the present custodians of the delightful Great Western 4mm scale, EM-gauge layout known as 'Cornwallis Yard'. Originally the work of the late Bob Haskins, 'Cornwallis' represents a fictional section of the GWR's Millbay branch in Plymouth circa 1935. Famous as a railhead for Ocean Liner traffic from America, with the GWR providing boat trains between Plymouth and Paddington, this setting allows the operation of a variety of passenger trains, different types of freight – and plenty of wagons to be shunted. The layout has a couple of unusual features, including the split-level display framed by a proscenium arch. On the upper level (looking from left to right) is part of Millbay Road station, a variety of trades and businesses along the back, with the goods depot and bonded store on the right. The lower level includes a small engine shed and a couple of carriage sidings.

Unfortunately Bob died suddenly in January 2004 before the whole layout was completed. However, with the aid of some remarkably thorough notes left behind, some of his friends were able to add several more planned buildings, and a working wagon hoist. This provides rail access between the two levels for goods trucks to be repaired in the wagon works alongside the line, using a method that is both space-efficient and interesting.

As has been chronicled elsewhere, Karl Crowther and Ian Worthington completed and exhibited the layout for a few years, at venues that Bob would have attended. We admired it on a number of occasions and asked for first refusal when they indicated that they might offer the layout for sale. So when the time came we welcomed the opportunity to ensure it remained on the exhibition circuit and honour the memory of Bob Haskins, a well-loved and talented modeller we did not know personally, but whose skills are much appreciated.

So it came to pass that in October 2008 we travelled from Southampton up to the Manchester Model Railway Society's exhibition in order to help man the layout, then bring half of it home in the back of our car after the show. With an invitation accepted for ExpoEM South in Portsmouth a few weeks later, we agreed that the two halves would be reunited when Karl brought the rest down south via Somerset... Indeed, when putting the layout together for the first time, we did so with the aid of photographs published in railway modelling magazine articles!

Amongst the paperwork handed over to us with the layout we discovered indications (dated 1998) that Bob's original intention had been to call the layout 'Collingwood Yard', and that it was to be set on a short, fictitious branch line running from the Great Western main line at Laira (just east of Plymouth) to

Two marvellous overall views looking down on the layout. Note how the buildings are at various angles, rather than all flat along the backscene. This adds to the authenticity of the layout in my opinion. *Both Steve Flint, courtesy of Railway Modeller*

Wembury on the South Devon coast. The notes also indicated that Bob had considered calling the lower level 'Bulwark Sidings'. It had certainly become 'Cornwallis Yard' by 2001, but without a separate name for the engine shed and carriage sidings area. Presumably the location had been moved to the Millbay Docks area of Plymouth by this time. Notes attached to Bob's sketches of the station building also suggest that he was considering a number of alternative names for it, including 'West Hoe Road', 'Citadel Road' and 'Bishops Place'. We have investigated these names and several do exist in the immediate locality. The only one that crossed the Millbay branch in reality was a Millbay Road (although by level crossing, not on a high-level bridge!), which might explain the ultimate naming decision.

The intriguingly designed signal box (noticeably wider than the tall brick pedestal on which it stands) is based on that at Yarnton, junction for Fairford on the Oxford, Worcester & Wolverhampton Railway north of Oxford. The engine shed model is based on a shortened version of that at Bullo Pill, between Lydney and Gloucester. The goods warehouse is based on Canons Marsh, with Millbay Road station modelled on Parson Street (both prototypes were in Bristol). Many of the other buildings are models of structures in the Plymouth and South Devon area. The wagon hoist may be loosely based on one of those at Birmingham Moor Street.

Bob's attention to detail in terms of research and creativity is still bearing fruit, inspiring the development of this layout from an end-to-end with a vertical cassette-based storage system into a continuous run with a sliding fiddle yard at the back. There was much thought and soul-searching before this decision was finally taken, but it came about in the belief that Bob could well have seen the operational potential of the change. Exhibiting experience soon yielded two inescapable truths to us, that the opportunity for decent lengths of both passenger and goods trains bound to and from his chosen location of Plymouth Docks was being limited by the cassette lengths, and that constant stock-handling risked potential damage.

This lineside view of the upper level is extremely realistic. Note the birds on top of the buildings. *Steve Flint, courtesy of Railway Modeller*

This low-level view shows the engine shed and its surroundings and the retaining wall. In fact, it is another of those photographs that, taken overall with the trains in it, makes a very realistic view that could again be taken for 'the real thing'. This is also in no small measure due to the skill of the photographer in composing the photograph. *Steve Flint, courtesy of Railway Modeller*

Operation requires three people, two of whom perform at the front of the layout. The main line is controlled from a free-standing control console (known to our team as the Wurlitzer!), which incorporates a 21-lever mechanical frame (sourced from Model Signal Engineering, built by Derek Mundy) for operating the points and signals. The levers, which are not interlocked, are connected to a bank of slide switches that supply power to the point and signal motors. A second operator controls and shunts the goods yard from an independent lever frame at the other end of the layout, while the third looks after the fiddle yard at the back. It is he/she who decides the sequence in which trains appear, as we do not currently run to a timetable. Obviously, cooperation between the team members is vital when transferring goods trains between the main line and yard via the loop.

One of the reasons for obtaining 'Cornwallis Yard' was that we had a large amount of EM-gauge locomotives and stock from a previous Great Western layout ('Doveford'). We also bought four additional locomotives and about 30 wagons with the layout, these all being fitted with Alex Jackson couplings, which are essential for shunting the goods yard. Our own stock is mostly fitted with three-link couplings, used on the through main-line trains. In its modified form, 'Cornwallis Yard' is fed by a seven-road traverser, each being able to hold two trains if required. We tend to run two long trains. One is the 'Ocean Liner Express', which will eventually be six coaches long (it is currently five, most of which are borrowed!).

This is normally hauled by a 'Castle' Class locomotive, which is the latest Hornby model converted to EM gauge with Alan Gibson wheels. The other long train is a goods, mainly vans, normally hauled by a Hornby '28xx' converted by carefully regauging the driving wheels with a specially made punch, turned up for the purpose by Phil Hall. The remaining trains are shorter, including an auto-train, several local passenger and short goods trains; recently a fish and perishables train has been added. The still growing stock of locomotives includes several pannier tanks of different classes, '45xx' and '4575' Class 2-6-2Ts, a '1361' Class 0-6-0ST and a 'Hall'. These should be joined during 2012 by several others, including a Southern Railway 'O2' for working transfer goods to the 'other' railway in Plymouth!

The low level (unofficially known as 'Bulwark Sidings') is fed from a three-road fiddle yard and is now totally independent of the upper level. The carriage sidings are used to display stock not used on the main layout, which includes a set of LMS coaches (from a Manchester to Plymouth working) and a variety of parcels vans and 'Siphons'. These can be shunted in and out from time to time, to change the display. A 'Cordon' gas tank wagon normally sits by the buffer stops. Mention must also be made of the unusual buffer stop on the longer siding, being an 'Iron Mink' van body with a buffer beam fitted halfway up the end; this is modelled on a prototype at Machynlleth, where there were two of them, now sadly removed.

There are obvious drawbacks in taking on someone else's work, especially in terms of electrical maintenance, but thankfully Bob left wiring schedules that cover most of the layout. Even answering questions about how the structures were made can often result in vague mumblings as we try to recall details of construction notes and magazine articles! We do know that many of the retaining walls, Millbay Road bridge and various other structures were built by Bob from polystyrene meat/pizza trays, scribed and painted with acrylics to represent the local stone. This novel method of construction resulted in a lighter (and cheaper!) finished creation, complemented by other structures made from foamboard and scrap pieces of card.

As originally built, the signals were operated by memory wire. When we took over the custodianship of the layout, several did not work satisfactorily (if at all), and over the following couple of years they became even more unreliable, despite attempts to bring them back to life. One of the earlier operators of the layout told us that they had all worked at one time, but not necessarily at the same time! The decision was made to replace the wire with miniature servos, and this was completed in time for the Blackburn exhibition in September 2011. This effort was rewarded at that show with 'Cornwallis Yard' being presented with the Model Signal Engineering trophy for signalling excellence, the second time that the trophy has come to the Southampton Model Railway Society, as it had been won by the club's 'Romsey' layout many years earlier.

While exhibiting we have occasionally been asked to explain why no attempts at landscaping are made on the extension round to the fiddle yard. This is largely due to the natural scenic breaks originally designed at either end of the main layout – and the question of how to match the quality of the work within the proscenium arch! Another more practical reason is that greater scenery depth causes transportation and storage difficulties. The layout in its present form fits into two cars with just enough room for overnight bags for the four operators. Any larger as a result of scenic end boards and it would be a hired van and a much greater cost for Exhibition Managers to bear.

And finally, internet ramblings yielded the fact that an American known as Colonel Robert Haskins served in the Revolutionary War at the Battle of Cornwallis in 1781. Was this known by Bob, influencing the layout name change…?

Black Hawk House (On30) described by Ian Drummond

Plan of 'Black Hawk House'

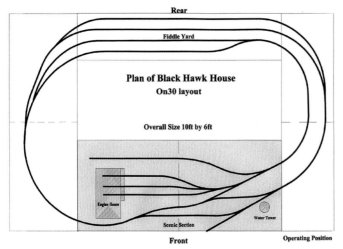

is Black Hawk House, which was in fact a converted barn, serving as the main engineering facility on the line. The main line climbs and curves round the engine house on a series of wooden trestles. One of the things I was keen to demonstrate on this layout was the scale of the mountains, and also the barrenness of the surroundings, particularly as most of the trees had been cut down for the mining industry.

The line is mainly operated by Bachmann Shays and Climaxes, although there is also a 'Galloping Goose' railcar on loan, and a couple of railtrucks. Operation of the layout is by a DCC system that allows for individual sound for each locomotive.

The visible part the layout is an attempt to model a prototypical American location in 7mm to the foot (On30) in a relatively small space. Black Hawk House was the engine house (American term for an engine shed) of the Gilpin Gold Tram, which served many of the mines of Gilpin County in Colorado, USA. This 2-foot-gauge line was constructed in several phases starting in 1887, and was eventually some 26 miles long. It twisted and climbed all over Gilpin County with steep gradients, in places at least 1 in 20, and sharp curves, the tightest of which was reputed to have been of 50 feet radius on the main line. Sadly the line was relatively short-lived, closing in 1917. A little bit of 'artistic licence' has taken place to allow the line to survive into the 1930s, having been purchased by a large mining company.

'Black Hawk House' is essentially a moving diorama with additional baseboards allowing a continuous run with fiddle yard; it measures 10 feet by 6 feet. At the centre of the diorama

A very good photograph of the locos on shed, the roof of which is extremely effective. I particularly like the 'Galloping Goose' in the foreground. *Ian Drummond*

This view shows the different levels on the layout to good effect. *Ian Drummond*

Nigel Adams now provides brief descriptions of five layouts he has built over the last few years.

Small MPD (O gauge) described by Nigel Adams

For this 1995 layout I had some bits left over from a Heljan engine shed kit that I had used on a previous layout and decided to see how small a layout I could build in O gauge – it measures just 45 by 22 inches. The engine shed was really the fiddle yard, and the length of the layout was decided by three factors: the main tracks should be 36 inches long to avoid cutting track as bought; the traverser should be 7½ inches long, which is quite long enough for the short-wheelbase locos I often use; and the layout should fit into the back of a Metro, which was the car I had at the time.

The backscene was an integral part of the baseboard, with shelves attached, and the control panel was built in so the layout was completely self-contained. It was exhibited at many shows and always attracted a great deal of interest because so much was fitted into such a small space, and yet it was an O-gauge layout.

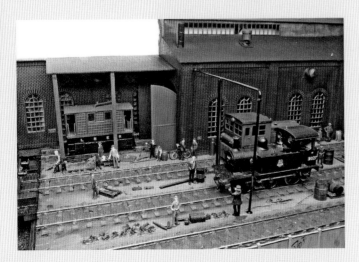

Like Colin French, for 'Small MPD' I used the Heljan engine shed kit – the larger one – as the basis of the layout. I used half of it to form what was effectively the hidden siding, and the remainder I used for the low-relief backscene. Note the detail, which I believe is essential on a small layout to keep the viewers' attention at shows. The end of the traverser can just be seen on the extreme left of the picture. *Martin Hewitt*

Extended MPD (O gauge) described by Nigel Adams

A corner of the extension to the 'Small MPD', showing scenic detail. This time I used the small Heljan engine shed as the basis for the extension and its low-relief backscene. *Martin Hewitt*

There is really not much to say about this 1999 layout except that I had so much pleasure from the 'Small MPD' that I doubled its size, to 90 by 22 inches! It had a separate control panel on the extension, which was joined electrically to the one on the original board via a plug and socket.

The extended layout was exhibited a number of times and was only broken up when I retired because I had no room for it. However, I salvaged all that I could in the way of buildings and scenic accessories and reused most of it on subsequent layouts.

A view of the small Heljan engine shed. The use of containers as storage is often seen in daily life but is not often modelled. Again, note the detail, especially the man in the hole talking to his colleagues. *Author*

The Shed Mk 2 (O gauge) described by Nigel Adams

This 2001 layout was totally self-contained and very similar to 'Small MPD' except that the main feature was a turntable instead of a traverser. It measured 45 by 22 inches plus an 8-inch extension on one track. Again Peco track was used. A cassette was used to transfer a loco from the visible part of the layout to the hidden siding behind the backscene.

Plan of 'The Shed' Mk 2

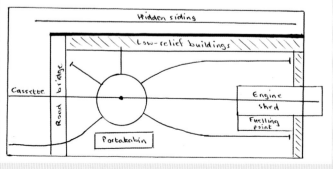

The feature of this layout was the turntable. Again the buildings are all from the Heljan small engine shed kit and I concentrated on scenic detail. *Martin Hewitt*

Scenic detail was again a major feature and the layout was exhibited at many shows where it always received favourable comment, especially from those who wanted to model in O gauge and had very little space.

Another view across the layout. Notice the orange temporary fence and the Fat Controller in the background, who is always an attraction for children at exhibitions. *Martin Hewitt*

The new feature for me was the mounting of all the switches on a piece of aluminium angle screwed to the backscene. I found this very effective and have done it on a number of layouts since.

Bottrill Street Yard (Mk 2) (O Gauge) described by Nigel Adams

Plan of 'Bottrill Street Yard (Mk 2)' *Courtesy BRM and Ian Wilson, Pacific Studios*

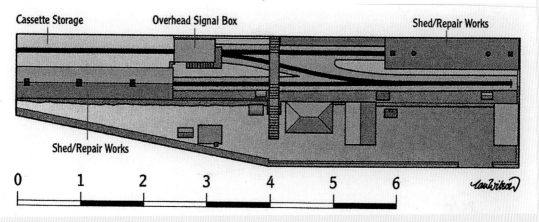

Cassette Storage   Overhead Signal Box   Shed/Repair Works

Shed/Repair Works

0   1   2   3   4   5   6

Not for the first time, for this 2003 project I went about designing the layout the wrong way round! A friend had two baseboard kits (each to build a board 48 by 12 inches), which he had had for ages and wanted to dispose of. I took them off his hands and

The 'scenic' board in front of the tracks was a later addition – it adds depth and gives the viewer something to 'look through'. It also provides an excuse to use some of the many excellent O-gauge vehicles available. In this case, the yard is used as a preserved bus storage area. *Tony Wright, courtesy of British Railway Modelling*

A close-up showing scenic detail: the bench outside the shed, the oil drums, the bike, the lamps and the steps up to the signal box. *Tony Wright, courtesy of British Railway Modelling*

had a happy time with Peco track and point templates devising a plan in O gauge that would fit the boards and give me operational interest. At a later stage I added a scenic board in front of each board to give extra depth, making the layout 24 inches deep at its widest point. It gives 'something to see past', which I think adds authenticity.

Again I used Heljan engine shed kit parts as well as parts from the Heljan signal box and footbridge kits. The added scenic boards at the front were deliberately not oblong and had various scenic detail 'cameos' on them; they were designed so that I could use some of my collection of road vehicles.

The layout could be operated using only locos (when it represented an engine shed) or locos and wagons when one of the buildings – which had the cassette area behind it – became a wagon repair shed.

Again the layout was regularly exhibited. It was called 'Bottrill Street Yard (Mk 2)' because I had already built a layout with that name and had had a 'nameboard' professionally made at a very reasonable price, and did not want to destroy it!

The Stabling Point (O Gauge) described by Nigel Adams

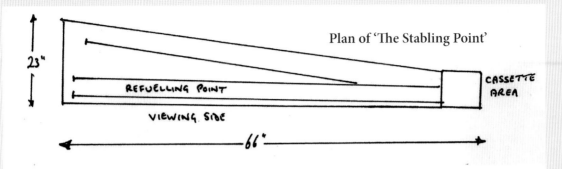

Plan of 'The Stabling Point'

23"

REFUELLING POINT

CASSETTE AREA

VIEWING SIDE

66"

This overall view is looking down on 'The Stabling Point' from above the bridge that disguises the exit to the cassette area. *Author*

Again, I built this 2011 layout to fit a baseboard rather the usual way of designing a layout then making the baseboard to suit the design. A fellow member of the Tywyn Model Railway Club, Bob Hey, had laid and wired the track for a layout and had then decided it was not really what he wanted, so he lifted the track and the baseboard was surplus. It was not the usual rectangular shape, being 54 inches long by 23 inches at its widest point excluding the cassette area, and that attracted me to it as I felt I could fit a diesel stabling point on it in 7mm scale (O gauge) to utilise the small diesels I have in my collection of rolling stock.

The unusual shape meant that it would be easy to design the layout to be operated from the front. Having done this on two occasions in the past, I found it worked well and wanted to do it again because it makes contact with the viewing public easier at exhibitions.

Bob had designed the baseboard to fold in half. That can still happen but, as I chose to have the rear track 'running away' from the viewer, it now folds into a parallelogram rather than an oblong. This is not a problem, but it is not necessary for me to fold it to transport it to shows at the moment as it will fit into my current car without being folded!

The design is very simple and uses only one point. As usual with me, I have concentrated on adding as much scenic detail as I can as I very much enjoy that side of our hobby. The stabling point is fed from a small cassette area, and it is very relaxing to shuffle locos around. At the moment I do not have an operating sequence, which is unusual for me; maybe I

will do so in the future. At the time of writing this there are no signals on the layout, but I have recently bought two colour light signals to fit in the near future.

The layout is quickly set up and dismantled at exhibitions and I only take one stock box with me. In the current economic climate (2012) it is an attraction to Exhibition Managers that the layout, and all that one has to take to an exhibition, fits into a Skoda Fabia saloon together with two operators and their overnight cases.

A ground-level view looking across the refuelling area. The yard lamps work (there are four of them). The use of short locos is a 'must' on a layout where the length of the scenic section is only 54 inches. *Author*

5 • Building prototype layouts
by Kevin Cartright

There are distinct advantages to using a real location as a basis for your layout. You are able to utilise all available information before any construction starts, and this research can be in the form of magazine articles, books, photographs, the internet – even visits to the site of the real thing, should it still be in existence, to give you information on your proposed layout. You should make sure that you obtain as much information as possible in order to achieve accuracy and to arrive at the end of your task feeling that you have done justice to the real thing. I find gathering knowledge of the subject not at all tedious; it actually adds to your satisfaction in your completed task. It can also save time and keeps guesswork to a minimum later in your model building.

I shall now endeavour to give you an insight as to how satisfying building prototypical layouts can be, using five examples.

'Seahouses'

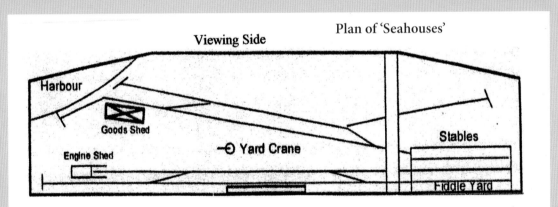

Plan of 'Seahouses'

'Seahouses', my first exhibition layout, was created almost by default after my wife bought me a kit of a North Eastern 'J71' as a Christmas present. This was my first foray into brass kit construction and the world of O gauge. I was very pleased with the finished loco in its black livery with red lining, as it looked good and also ran extremely well. I was now smitten with this gauge and scale.

Having built the 'J71', I had a dilemma – where to run it? This was soon resolved for me with the purchase of a small Oakwood Press book called *The North Sunderland Railway*, which was discovered on a second-hand stall at the Warley Club's Harry Mitchell Centre show in the days before the NEC, and cost me the princely sum of 50p!

On returning home I found a diagram of my 'J71' on page 17. What a revelation this little book was to me – a complete history of a small privately owned branch line running from Chathill on the East Coast Main Line to

These four photographs speak for themselves, and represent all that this book is about – realistic railway modelling. A non-modeller who saw them was amazed when told they were pictures of a model railway, which is a great compliment to Kevin Cartwright and to Tony Wright, the photographer. *All Tony Wright, courtesy of British Railway Modelling*

Seahouses, a small fishing port on the North East coast! There were track plans for both Chathill and Seahouses stations, diagrams and sizes for all the station buildings, and drawings of all the locos and rolling stock that ran on the line. The book contained almost everything I needed to know about this little-known branch line, which sadly closed in 1951. There were pages of very informative photographs, giving me an insight into the vehicles used around the station yard and the diagrams for the buildings, etc. I had found my prototypical layout!

At this stage a start can be made on building the layout, as you should now have in your mind's eye what the layout could or indeed should look like based on the information you have collated. In my case, 'Seahouses' had started with the building of a locomotive, so I decided to build all the rest of the rolling stock and locomotives required for this railway. That amounted to eight locos, nine coaches, three

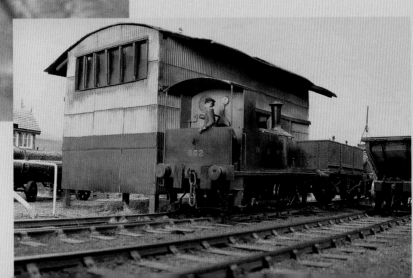

brake-vans and 20 wagons, although this was far more that actually ran on the line at any one time, as there would have been only two locos in steam daily, but I thought that some variety in rolling stock was called for at exhibitions.

At the time of building 'Seahouses' none of the stock was available in ready-to-run form, so I spent the best part of the next five years sourcing and constructing the rolling stock. This was, I hasten to add, as well as working full time in the fire service and doing all the little jobs that wives find for us to do! The building of the stock was perhaps the most tedious part of this project.

I then turned to the construction of the buildings. The station building, engine shed, goods shed, stables and fish dock were all built from studying drawings in the aforementioned little book. These prototype buildings would have been made from corrugated metal formed off-site, then assembled on-site as required. The model buildings were constructed mostly from Slaters corrugated Plastikard over a plain Plastikard inner shell to give stability. The colours of the buildings were mostly decided by me as there are only black and white images available, but these gave me to believe that the buildings were two-tone with a darker bottom and a lighter top. All were detailed inside and illuminated, as the finished layout would be depicted during both the hours of daylight and at nightfall. The buildings took me six months to complete.

As the town of Seahouses was, and still is to some extent, a fishing port, some form of harbour was required with, of course, a selection of prototypical boats to adorn it. These took the form of a Clyde 'Puffer' and two fishing boats. Again these took some time to research, source and build. The smaller fishing boat was a wooden-plank-on-frame kit, while the larger boat and the Clyde 'Puffer' were scratch-built. The latter came into being by using the freeze frame on the VCR to make drawings of the Clyde 'Puffer' used in an old TV series called *The Tales of Para Handy*, which was named *The Vital Spark* – my recreation was called *The Coiled Sock*. The large fishing boat was called *The Lady Judith* after my wife, and the smaller one just had its

port identifying letters and numbers. The total time for this task was four months.

A word of warning! As you will by now have gathered, 'Seahouses' took me a considerable amount of time to construct. In fact, from the idea first raising its head until I had a finished layout was getting on for eight years. It should be remembered that every item built and every task on this layout was done by me except for some help and advice on the wiring. Remember also that this is a hobby and time deadlines and limitations should have no place in our recreations of miniature worlds. If perhaps a certain piece of construction does not go to plan or, heaven forbid, is a total disaster, the next time that you attempt it you will have learned something from before that makes it more successful. I personally do not work to deadlines and allow things to evolve naturally to a certain extent. It is for me purely a very enjoyable hobby, although I appreciate that some people do not share this opinion. Of course, all layouts take differing times to complete, especially if there are several people working on different aspects of it. These days, with so much good ready-to-run stock available as well as a myriad of buildings and vehicles from which to choose, I feel sure that a good layout could be completed in less than a year.

Some people would say that to alter the original to suit the model would make the layout not prototypical. I suppose technically that is true. However, in the railway modelling world we may have to work to constraints and logistics such as the space that we have available to build the layout, the size of the vehicle we intend to use if exhibiting it, and altering it to create more interesting operation at exhibitions, and so on.

In the case of 'Seahouses' a few alterations were made from the original, the main one being that I ran the line down to the harbour-side fish-loading dock. In reality, the harbour was almost half a mile from the station down a hill, the fish being transported by road from the harbour to the station. The main reason for the railway at Seahouses was to transport fish caught there to the main North Eastern cities and market towns in a reasonable time. This separation of railway and harbour unfortunately could not be accommodated on the layout, as it would have made the length more than 40 feet, not perhaps a good idea when the layout was operated just by me and my wife!

The next alteration was the addition of a second run-round loop on the goods siding, with a spur to the stables. The general rule on alterations to a prototype is to try not to make too many of them, or you will end up with something that looks nothing like the original.

Having now made all the buildings, rolling stock, boats, etc, and having acquired or made all the trackwork and points required, I now had to make a plan of the layout that would accommodate all of the aforementioned models and track. This was done on my front drive on a sunny summer's day with the use of a roll of old wallpaper pinned together at various places, and all the buildings, boats and track placed in their appropriate positions using information from my trusty book.

After many hours and mugs of tea, all the positions were marked on the wallpaper, which was then used as a template for cutting the baseboards. I ended up with three boards of 6 feet by 2ft 4in, with folding legs built in, making a total scenic layout 18 feet long, which I suppose is an average size for an O-gauge layout, although a great deal shorter in length than the prototype.

As you can see, the layout does not have to be exactly the same as the prototype in order to create a convincing model. If it *looks* right, then it probably *is* right. You may not ever get to the end of a project if you are constantly altering how you want the finished model to look. My wife tells me that I am very fortunate in that I have a very clear view of what the finished layout/project will look like well before I am approaching the end. I am sure she is right and that this is an advantage because, as I previously said, you must have some idea of the finished result quite early on.

'Seahouses' was not an elaborate layout. The track plan was essentially two run-round loops, one serving the station and fish dock with the other serving the goods yard,

harbour, coaling jetty and stables. Both were accessed from a hidden four-road sector plate at one end of the layout. However, the layout was about a lot more than the track plan.

'A railway ran to it.' This was a model of part of the fishing port of Seahouses complete with a station, some of the harbour and of course the boats. The layout also featured more than 200 highly detailed figures in various small dioramas set into the layout. The backscene was quite plain but effective, featuring a grey stormy day over the North Sea with Bamburgh Castle in the distance.

'Seahouses' was always going to be an exhibition layout, and as such I wanted it to be something totally different from what was 'on the circuit' at the time. I endeavoured to bring other aspects to the railway modelling world such as marine modelling, vehicles, figure-painting, etc. This was all brought together at its very first show at the Bonded Warehouse in Stourbridge in 1998. The layout was presented under a grey/green material canopy to cut out any unwanted venue lighting. Under this canopy were the lights, which could be controlled to give representations of day or night operation, with all buildings, boats and harbour lights illuminated. When I stood back and looked at my creation after we had finished setting it up, I knew that all my hard work had been truly worth it.

After 85 exhibitions and many awards I made the decision to part with 'my baby', as my wife called it. We were moving to Devon from the Midlands and did not have the space to store the layout. I would like to think that 'Seahouses' had some small influence on the model railway scene as there are quite a few layouts now with both harbours and boats on them. Also, there are kits of boats available now, even a Clyde 'Puffer'! And yes, I have at last visited Seahouses. There is a plaque on the car park wall that tells you that there was once a railway there, and we even found a walk along the original trackbed.

However, 'onwards and upwards', as they say. The next layouts/projects were already in my imagination.

'Stodmarsh'

Plan of 'Stodmarsh'

'**S**todmarsh' has, to date, completed around 25 shows on the exhibition circuit. It is an O-gauge model of a proposed, but never built, extension from Wingham to Canterbury in Kent. Although it never existed in reality and is therefore rather outside the parameters of this chapter, this small layout looks very convincing.

As with the 'Seahouses' photographs, these views of 'Stodmarsh' by Craig Tiley exemplify in practice what we are trying to say in this book about the importance of scenic detail. Every time you look at them, you can see how the detail comes together to make a whole scenic picture. *All Craig Tiley, courtesy of Model Rail*

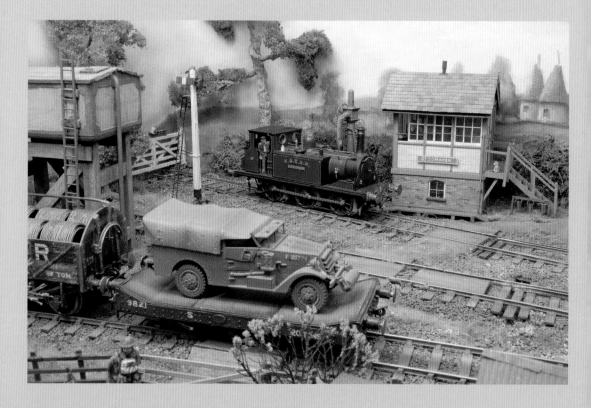

I only mention it because it shows that you do not necessarily need a prototype to build a convincing model railway, so long as you adopt some of the ideas and techniques mentioned in these paragraphs, for example ideas from prototypes incorporated into fictional railway locations surrounded perhaps by actual locations such as Stodmarsh, which is a small village in Kent. This fictional model railway type of modelling is made all the more pleasurable when someone at an exhibition says, 'I used to stand on that bridge trainspotting when I was a boy.' I still haven't had the heart to say that the bridge or location never existed! However, in my opinion it is one of the best compliments you will receive for your modelling efforts.

'Arley'

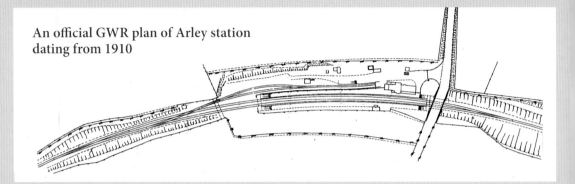

An official GWR plan of Arley station dating from 1910

At the time of writing, this OO-gauge layout is yet to appear on the exhibition circuit as the baseboards are not constructed. Following my normal method of construction, all the buildings, bridges and other structures are completed, and I also have all the rolling stock ready.

The research for 'Arley' needed a different approach from that adopted for 'Seahouses', for, unlike the station at Seahouses, Arley is still in existence on the preserved Severn Valley Railway, and was only 18 miles from our home at the time in the Midlands. My wife and I spent many happy hours on Arley station with our two 'Westies', Dougal and Hamish, watching the trains go by in all weathers. This is probably our favourite station in England.

During our many and frequent visits the whole station was measured up, as was the Harbour Inn just down the road, the road bridge over the track and, just over a mile

Above: This is an absolutely stunning picture! It also shows the photographer's skill. It is a photograph of Kevin's model of Victoria Bridge taken at dusk overlooking Brixham Harbour. You just cannot tell that it is not real! People who have seen it have difficulty accepting that it is a 'composite' photograph. *Craig Tiley, courtesy of Model Rail*

Left: The model of Victoria Bridge, which is slightly shortened to enable it to fit on the layout baseboards. It is made from plasticard and Das clay on a plywood base. *Kevin Cartwright*

Above: **A good early view of Arley station showing the main station building, signal box, road bridge and original high starter signal. Note that the platform shelter is not yet built and the contractors are building the platform extension in front of the signal box.** *Kevin Cartwright collection*

Right: **Arley station, now part of the preserved Severn Valley Railway, is seen in the summer of 1999.** *Kevin Cartwright*

down the track, the famous Victoria Bridge.

I have taken hundreds of photographs over the years but, even with an existing preserved station, care should be taken, as in some instances buildings have been altered from the original you wish to model, or buildings not original to the site have been moved there from other locations. I found that the signal box now in use at Arley was not the original, but the one in use at Highley station just down the line was almost identical apart from the fact that the steps up to it were on the opposite side of the box. I built the steps on the correct side for Arley, but now – wouldn't you know it – there is a ready-built signal box that can be purchased!

'Arley' was intended to be complete by now, as some of the structures were built at the same time that I was modelling 'Seahouses'. However, some life-changing developments, including retirement from my career in the fire service and moving to Brixham in Devon to run a guest house, interrupted my modelling for a couple of years.

Although our beautiful Victorian seafront home is huge, it does not have a garage or even a garden in which to place a shed, so of course I am limited to what I can achieve, and as a result several projects have been mothballed for a while. We now also have a small house back in the Midlands, which my wife reckons we bought because I liked the garage! The said

The replacement signal box at Arley. *Kevin Cartwright*

The model of the original signal box. The one that is there now is not the same type. *Kevin Cartwright*

garage is now filling up with baseboards and the like!

As 'Arley' is a 'through' branch-line station, the layout is to be a 'tail-chaser' in the form of a long oval that will allow trains to pass in the station area. No compromise will be made on the scale length of the layout, with the exception of Victoria Bridge, which has been built slightly shortened, but is still large enough to encompass the river scene, an important part of the layout.

'Arley' will not be as time-consuming as 'Seahouses' in that full use is to be made of all that is available in ready-to-run locos and

rolling stock, with the addition of a lot of my kit-built GWR stock built many years ago for my OO-gauge layout 'Burland Heights', which ran around the whole of the loft in our previous house.

I hope you enjoy the pictures of the buildings in this section, as they are models in their own right, mainly constructed from card with individually placed bricks attached. The exception to this is Victoria Bridge, which is constructed from plasticard and Das clay. I have not discussed any of the modelling techniques used as that is an entire subject in its own right.

Arley station building, platform shelter and weighbridge hut. *All Kevin Cartwright*

The road bridge over the line. *Kevin Cartwright*

'Brixham Bay'

This is an unexpected research project that has led to an N-gauge prototypical layout that is almost ready to be exhibited. It came into being simply because of my wife's interest in N-gauge rolling stock and buildings. While I have been demonstrating modelling techniques in O and OO at various shows over the years, she decided that she would build some N-gauge items. She started with some Ratio buildings, then joined

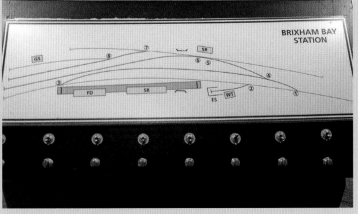

Plan of 'Brixham Bay' on the control panel. *Kevin Cartwright*

the N Gauge Society and built some N-gauge trucks that looked rather nice on completion.

My intention in the beginning was to help her construct a small N-gauge layout to use the bits she had built, and also some of the readily available products for this scale. However, after our move to Brixham I soon found the local bookshop on the Quay and what did I find on the railway bookshelf? Another Oakwood Press book, this one called *The Brixham Branch Railway*. By this time I

had decided that my wife's small layout would have to be put on the back burner, as this other far more interesting project had presented itself to me.

I did recall reading an article some time ago in the *Great Western Journal* that went into great detail about this little branch line. My next task was to find out where exactly the station had been located, as it closed in 1961. I soon found the site of the railway high above the port overlooking the harbour, although,

Above: The part-built layout in its 'box'. The flap at the front is hinged and closes for transport. *Kevin Cartwright*

Right: An overall view of the layout under construction with the backscene removed. The trackbed has been removed for wiring, the school is in position on the playground and most other completed buildings are just standing on the station forecourt. *Kevin Cartwright*

Furzeham School is beginning to take shape, with the trackbed and the hand-painted backscene behind it. Kevin is a superb artist as well as a superb modeller, but he is very reticent about his artistic skills! *Kevin Cartwright*

sadly from my point of view, the site was now covered in a housing estate, the car park for Furzeham School and tennis courts. However, all the station abutments were still there, as was the road bridge at the far end of the station platform. I even found the brick base of the signal box incorporated in a larger wall. Most of the surrounding buildings are still there and I have had a fine time trying to discover which ones were in existence at the time that I am modelling. Most of the houses, etc, surrounding the railway were built at the turn of the century.

Using the *Great Western Journal* information, the Oakwood Press book and my own measurements of the station site, the distance from the station throat to the buffer stops came out at 9 feet for an N-gauge layout. Unfortunately, the length I had to work with was 7 feet, so compromises had to be made, as had been the case with 'Seahouses'.

I have spent many hours toiling up the hill to the station site, as the school next to the station is still in existence. However, I had to obtain permission from the Headmistress to

Brixham station under construction. *Kevin Cartwright*

photograph the building and prove to her that I had no ulterior motives! What a world we live in today! As I write this, I am completing the school, although this again is a building that has been added to over the years and has proved difficult to research for the period I am modelling.

As I have nowhere in the guest house to construct baseboards, these were built for me to my design by a friend. What has actually been constructed is a box, 7 feet by 2ft 6in by

1ft 6in, with a viewing slot in the front. I built the station buildings, etc, mostly from plasticard. On taking delivery of my box, I decided on a viewing point that is not much modelled – it would be viewed from the station approach rather than from the trackside.

There were a couple of reasons for this decision. First, I was finding that N-gauge couplings seem too long for the vehicles to which they are attached and, as far as I am concerned, spoil the look of the ready-to-run locos and rolling stock available, but are obviously totally necessary to the running of a model railway. By having the layout base 4 feet from the ground, the trackbed approximately 1ft 6in from the front of the layout, and the station building, engine shed and boundary walls obscuring most of the loco and rolling stock wheels and couplings, the problem was all but solved. Painting the couplings the same colour as the ballasting makes them almost invisible at the viewing length (approximately

Brixham goods shed. *Kevin Cartwright*

Brixham signal box with one of the handmade working signals. (Remember this is N gauge!) *Kevin Cartwright*

2 feet), yet fully functional for coupling/uncoupling shunting operations.

The second reason for this viewing point was purely pictorial. The layout is called 'Brixham Bay'. If the layout were viewed from the trackside, no one would be able to see anything of Brixham or the bay owing to the high location of the railway above the town. At the period being modelled there would have been just the school and fields beyond.

The third reason is that, as the railway was high above the town, this would not be apparent if modelled from the trackside. However, from the station approach I could get away from the 'flat earth' scenario and place the model as it should be, incorporating all the different ground levels of the prototype as well as its position relative to the town as painted in the backscene.

I thought long and hard about the backscene. This was made a lot more complicated by turning round the viewing direction, as I have just discussed. Initially I took lots of pictures of the vista across the bay from what was the station location, then I joined these together to give me something to work from. I then had again to decide what buildings were in existence at the period being modelled. I decided to collate all this information on to an oil painting curved at the ends to fit my box. I used a piece of hardboard to which I attached a roll of canvas, and this formed my backscene. I have been painting this on my easel for more than six months and it is now almost complete – much to my wife's relief! I should mention at this point that I do have a talent for painting, which is one of the reasons I chose to undertake this method of forming my backscene. I am hoping that it will look pretty spectacular when all is complete! However, usually the simpler the backscene the more your modelling creations in front of it will stand out, so if you are not a budding Picasso it really does not matter!

'Brixham Bay' is now almost complete with the board/box made, the buildings constructed, locos and stock purchased, the school building nearing completion and the backscene painted. All that is left to do is the wiring and lighting. This layout has taken me about two years to construct and should be ready for exhibition shortly.

'Ventnor West'

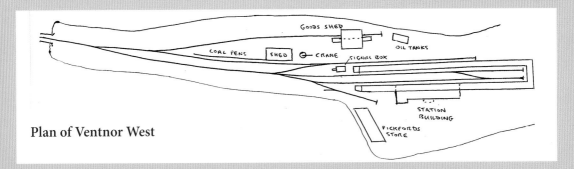

Plan of Ventnor West

Making a model of Ventnor West (not to be confused with the other station, simply called Ventnor) on the Isle of Wight came into my mind while there visiting relatives. My wife's cousin lives in a bungalow built on the site of the original signal box for Ventnor West. The station building is still intact to a certain extent, although it has been used as a private residence for several years. There was also a lovely little transhipment warehouse next to the station, used by Pickfords when the railway was still in existence; sadly this has been demolished quite recently. This project seemed too good an opportunity to miss when I had all the information in front of me.

Before we moved to Devon we spent many holidays on the island and I would set off across the road, armed with my drawing pad and measuring tape, to visit the elderly couple who lived at the station. I began to collate the information needed for this prototypical layout. Getting the scale correct for the buildings was relatively simple as some were still there, and I acquired more information from books found in a second-hand bookshop and from Havenstreet station, which is the

The original: Ventnor West station. *Kevin Cartwright collection*

Below: The model: the station building was constructed from high-quality thick card with stonework made using Das compound. The building is awaiting final detailing and weathering. *Kevin Cartwright*

hub of the island's preserved line. I was also able to photograph some of the island's rolling stock at Havenstreet, and began to build the locos needed for the project.

At the time of writing, the boards and all the buildings are now complete, as is most of the rolling stock. Unfortunately the elderly gentleman has passed away and I feel sure that the station building's days are numbered, in its present form at least. I feel very fortunate to have been able to gain so much information from the horse's mouth, as it were. It is not very often that such information is available these days.

In the future you may see some or all of these layouts on the exhibition circuit and remember reading about them. I very much hope so.

Ventnor West signal box. *Kevin Cartwright collection*

Above: The other end of the station building. When modelling prototypes careful thought must be given as to whether you have the space – the model of Ventnor West station is more than 3 feet long! *Kevin Cartwright*

Below: The model of Ventnor West signal box, scratch-built using plasticard. 7mm scale allows the builder to incorporate a lot of fine interior detail. *Both Kevin Cartwright*

Prototype layouts require prototype locomotives and rolling stock, which is a separate subject not covered in this chapter. Here is 'Terrier' loco No 13 *Carisbrooke*, which will be prototypically correct to run on 'Ventnor West' when it is completed. *Kevin Cartwright*

Left: 'Terrier' No 8 *Freshwater* on the layout. *Kevin Cartwright*

Below: The 'driving end' of push-pull set No 484 having an outing on Kevin's 'Stodmarsh' layout. *Kevin Cartwright*

I am well aware that space is major consideration in modern houses, not just for a layout but for somewhere to make one's models. Some very ingenious solutions to finding a suitable workbench space have been described in the model railway press over the years, and one that always attracted me was that used by the late John Hillman, who was one of the founder members of the Tywyn & District MRC in 2001.

As my wife and I do now, he lived in a two-bedroom bungalow where space was at a premium. His solution was to use a bureau, which he had bought second-hand but was in good condition. The huge advantage of a bureau is that it has drawers on either side in which to store things, and the 'cubby holes' in the work area can be used for small tools, etc. What is more, when you stop work you can just shut the bureau 'lid' and everything in the room is tidy!

For many years my bench was a computer desk, which our two sons had used when they were at school. We were going to dispose of it until I realised its potential as a bench. The only additions I made were two small trays for storing small tools such as files, pliers and screwdrivers. It served me well and, when we moved to our bungalow, I donated it to our club, where it is still in use (see the photograph on page 9).

One of the advantages of being a vicar is that vicarages and rectories almost always have at least four bedrooms. In my years as a vicar I always used the smallest bedroom as my modelling room – both for my layout and my workspace. I was fortunate in being able to do this when I retired, even though our cottage only had three bedrooms.

On 'downsizing' to a two-bedroom bungalow recently this became impossible,

Two views of the small desk that is now my bench. *Author*

and the only alternatives were a ready-boarded loft or a shed in the garden, which was in need of major repairs.

I took advice and was told that the shed could be made sound and habitable. It already had mains electricity to it. For a lot less than the cost of a new one, I now have a shed 12 feet by 8 feet with a new roof and a new floor; it has insulated walls, floor and roof, and is lined with plywood. It has also been rewired

The shed. The fact that it has no windows does not cause a problem. (In any case, many layouts are in lofts that have no windows!) *Author*

The storage unit on the right is from Ikea, 'topped' by plywood. The shelves at the end I put up, and a Gu15 layout on an ironing board is stored underneath. The 'folding trolley' in the centre is very useful at exhibitions. *Author*

and fitted with extra power points and new lighting. I fitted a carpet very cheaply using an offcut from the local carpet supplier. I saw a small desk in our local second-hand shop, which was just what I was looking for and it only cost me £15!

My elder son queried the removal of the windows, but it has not proved to be a problem. If it is not raining the door can be retained in one of two open positions. If it is raining the door is kept shut or I stay indoors! The insulation of the walls, floor and roof has made a huge difference to the temperature in the shed. We have had some really hot weather and the shed remained very cool; conversely,

when it is cold, the insulation keeps the heat in. The only means of heating is a tubular heater, supplemented by a fan heater if it is really cold, but it does not have to stay on for long.

If you have the choice between a shed or a loft as I did, I can recommend a well-insulated shed. Our loft is well insulated, but still suffers from extremes of weather. The shed is also far better for access and you do not have to get layouts and equipment up and down a loft ladder through a relatively small hatch. The older you get, climbing up and down loft ladders with layouts and equipment is an activity you can do without!

Index

Adams, Nigel 49, 117-122
Alderman, Bob 64-67

Bala Lake Railway 37, 39
Ballasting 78-79
Barker, David and Alison 111-115
Baseboards 66, 68, 79-80, 103
Beaches, modelling 47
Bennett, Stan 53, 54
Boats, modelling 57, 126, 127
Bowyer, Nigel 31
Bragg, Mike 48, 89-96
Branch lines, layouts based on 22, 25
Breweries, modelling 83
'Building blocks', layout design concept 23
Buildings 57, 66, 70, 73, 74, 126, 135, 138-139
Burgess, Neil 101-104
Burnard, Jack 71-74

Camping sites, modelling 47
Canals, modelling 46, 56, 90, 91-92
Cards, as operating system 83
Cartwright, Kevin 50, 57, 122ff
Cassettes, use of as fiddle yard 113, 118, 121, 122
Church, David 12
'Clutter', modelling 24, 35-36
Cole, Mike 104, 105
Collieries, layouts based on 17; modelling 29, 58-59, 71-74
Conveyors, modelling 59, 73-74
Cox, M. J. 21
Crowther, Karl 111

Denny, Peter 7, 25
Docks and harbours, layouts

based on 17, 123-127; modelling 32, 57
Drummond, Ian 57, 109-110, 116-117
Dyer, Frank 8

Eagles, Norman 27
East Riding Finescale Group 67

Factories and industrial, layouts based on 17; modelling 30-31, 105-109
Fiddle yards 64, 69, 70, 72, 82, 99
Figures, modelling 25, 48, 50, 59, 108
Flynn, Hugh 78-79
'Framing' of layouts 65, 80, 97, 111, 127
Freezer, Cyril 27, 40
French, Colin 82-88
Front of layout, operating from 65, 66, 81

Gelsthorpe, Derek 46
Goss, Peter 70
Gravett, Gordon and Maggie 42-43

Harvey, Peter 76, 77
Haskins, Bob 111-115
Hey, Bob 121
Heywood, Sir Arthur 11
Hull MRC 93

Ironing board, as baseboard 13

Jenkinson, David 103

Kelly, Maurice 27, 28
Koester, Tony 23
Kyle of Lochalsh 21

Layouts

82G 4, 61-63
Allied Marine and Locomotive Company 23
Arley 130-133
Ashwood Basin 91-92
Balls Yard 82
Bank Hall Sidings 56, 74-75
Black Hawk House 116-117
Borchester Market 8
Bottrill Street Yard Mk 1 8; Mk 2 119-120
Box Street 90
Brixham Bay 133-137
Brookhurst 8
Buckingham Branch 7, 25
Cheapside Depot 10, 11
Chee Tor 7
Chiltern Green 7
Cornwallis Yard 60, 111-115
Craig & Mertonford Railway 8
Cripple Corner 44
Dagnall End 47
Ditchling Green 43
Dock Green Loco 85
Dudley Road 77
Extended MPD 118
Ffodos Loco 84
Ffodos Road 84
Ffodos Treacle Works 85-86
Foxbile Brewery 86-87
Gas Works 2-3, 45, 64-67
George Street Stabling Point Mk 1 55, 79-80; Mk 2 51, 81
Haslington MPD 53
Hospital Gates 67-71
Howards Bank 54

Idle Way 46
Iron Street Sheds 11, 13, 48
Ledsam Street Yard 82-83
Lenches Bridge 48, 89-90
Lochnagar 99-101
Melbury Loops 22-23
Merlinwood 104-105
Mullacombe 27, 48
Napier Street 31
Neptune Road Depot 11, 12
North Hetton Colliery 58-59, 71-74
North Plains 98-99
Pattingham 93-94
Pempoul Reseau Breton 42
Peters Street Station 76
Polhendra Clay Works 78-79
St Minions 93
Seahouses 57, 123-127
Shed, The 49, 118-119
Sherwood Section of the LMS 27
Small MPD 117
Spinners End 95-96
Stabling Point, The 49, 121-122
Stodmarsh 1, 5, 50, 128-129, 140
Teesside Steel 51, 105-109
Tolcarn Engine Shed 52
Tremore 96-98
Tywyn Railway Preservation Society 11, 14, 15
Ventnor West 137-140
Wagon Works, The 87-88
Warmley 101-104
Waterhulme 57, 109-110
Widnes Vine Yard 25
Winton 25-26, 40
Works, The 11, 12, 13
Works Yard, The 18-20
Worthington Shed 10

Leek & Manifold Railway 109-110

Levels, use of different 54, 55, 60, 65, 111, 114, 115
Lights, dimming 58, 67, 127
Loco sheds, layouts based on 10-11, 14, 15, 16, 17-18, 77, 85, 117-119; modelling 33, 34, 41, 52, 53, 61-63

Machynlleth 16
Manchester MRC 111
Military railways 32, 71, 104
Milton Railway Group 22
Murray, Mark 51, 81

Narrow gauge, layouts based on 22, 109-110; modelling 31, 32, 39
New Cross Gate 18-21
Normanton & Pontefract RMS 79-80
North Sunderland Railway 123

Oxford MRC 27

Paignton & Dartmouth Steam Railway 34, 37
Palette, Nick 96-101
Parkinson, John 41
Pearce, Bill 74-75
Plans, full-size 73, 127
Pomroy, John 25-26, 40
Preserved railways, modelling 11-12, 15, 34, 36-37
Prototypes, layouts based on 22

Redditch MRC 47
Ripley, Neil 67-71, 93
Ross, John 104-105

Scott, Richard 55, 79-80
Sector plates 64, 65, 72, 82
Severn Valley Railway 34, 130
Sheds, garden, use of 8, 141-142
Shunters, diesel 29-31
Sibley, Alan 23

Sidings, layouts based on 17, 74
Signal boxes, modelling 113, 132, 139
Smith Nigel 61-63
Somerset & Dorset Railway 103, 104
Stabling points, modelling 10, 49, 79-81
Steelworks, modelling 105

Talyllyn Railway 11, 35, 43
Termini, layouts based on 22, 76
Timetables, for model railways 26-27
Trackwork 66, 73, 75, 78
Transportation of exhibition layouts 68, 76, 122, 134
Traversers 42, 117
Trollope, Jack 90
Turntables 67, 88, 95, 119
Tywyn MRC 10, 121, 141

USA, layouts based on 98-99, 116-117

Vehicles, modelling 25, 38, 49, 59, 74; buses 38, 120
Viewpoints 65, 136-137

Wagon works, modelling 31, 44, 87-88
Wass, John 70
Wetherall, Jeff 104-109
Whittingham Hospital Railway 67, 68, 70
Winding, Peter F. 18-21
Woodyards, modelling 27, 28
Workbenches 9, 141
Worthington, Ian 111
Wright, Keith 44

Yards, layouts based on 17, 82-83; modelling 60
Yeend, Terry 52
Yeovil MRG 45, 64-67